Adlerian, Cognitive, and Constructivist Therapies

An Integrative Dialogue

**Richard E. Watts, PhD,** is associate professor and director of the counseling program in the Department of Educational Psychology at Baylor University, in Waco, Texas. He received his PhD in counseling from the University of North Texas in 1994. Prior to joining the Baylor faculty in 2000, Dr. Watts held faculty positions at Texas A & M University–Commerce and at Kent State University. Dr. Watts has authored over 50 professional articles and book chapters, 3 books, and currently serves on the editorial boards of several professional journals. His current interests include Adlerian, cognitive, and constructive approaches to individual and couple and family counseling, counselor supervision and counselor efficacy, ethical and legal issues, play therapy, and religious and spirituality issues in counseling.

Adlerian, Cognitive, and Constructivist Therapies

An Integrative Dialogue

Richard E. Watts, PhD, Editor

 Springer Publishing Company

Copyright © 2003 by Springer Publishing Company, Inc.

All rights reserved

No part of this publication may be reproduced, stored in a retrieval system, or transmitted in any form or by any means, electronic, mechanical, photocopying, recording, or otherwise, without the prior permission of Springer Publishing Company, Inc.

Springer Publishing Company, Inc.
536 Broadway
New York, NY 10012-3955

Acquisitions Editor: Sheri W. Sussman
Production Editor: Sara Yoo
Cover design by Joanne Honigman

03 04 05 06 07 / 5 4 3 2 1

Library of Congress Cataloging-in-Publication Data

Adlerian, cognitive, and constructivist therapies: an integrative dialogue/ Richard E. Watts, editor
    p. cm.
    Includes bibliographical references and index.
    ISBN 0-8261-1984-0
    1. Counseling. 2. Psychotherapy. 3. Adlerian psychology. I. Watts, Richard E.
BF637.C6A335 2003
    150.19'53—dc21   2003042570

Printed in the United States of America by Maple-Vail Book Manufacturing Group.

Contents

Contributors	vii
Foreword by Gerald Corey	ix
Acknowledgments	xi

Chapter 1	An Introduction to the Dialogue *Richard E. Watts*	1

Part 1: Adlerian and Constructivist Psychotherapies

Chapter 2	Integrating Adlerian and Constructive Therapies: An Adlerian Perspective *Richard E. Watts and Bernard H. Shulman*	9
Chapter 3	Adlerian and Constructivist Psychotherapies: A Constructivist Perspective *John V. Jones, Jr. and William J. Lyddon*	38

Part 2: Adlerian and Cognitive Psychotherapies

Chapter 4	Commonalities Between Adlerian Psychotherapy and Cognitive Therapies: An Adlerian Perspective *Len Sperry*	59
Chapter 5	Adlerian Psychology and Cognitive-Behavioral Therapy: A Cognitive Therapy Perspective *Arthur Freeman and June Urschel*	71

Part 3: Cognitive, Adlerian, and Constructivist Responses

Chapter 6　Adlerian, Cognitive-Behavioral, and Constructivist Psychotherapies: Commonalities, Differences, and Integration
E. Thomas Dowd　91

Chapter 7　A Cognitive Conundrum: Where's the Thinking in Cognitive?
Michael P. Maniacci　107

Chapter 8　Two Paths Diverge in a Wood: Cognitive–Constructivist Contrasts and the Future Evolution of Adlerian Psychotherapy
Robert A. Neimeyer　122

Index　*139*

Contributors

Gerald Corey, EdD, ABPP
Professor Emeritus of Human
 Services
California State University,
 Fullerton
Fullerton, CA

E. Thomas Dowd, PhD, ABPP
Interim Department Chairperson
Department of Psychology
Kent State University
Kent, OH

Arthur Freeman, EdD, ABPP
Chairman and Professor
Philadelphia College of
 Osteopathic Medicine
Adler School of Professional
 Psychology
Philadelphia, PA

John V. Jones, Jr., PhD, LPC, NCC, ACT
Associate Professor
St. Edwards University
Austin, TX

William J. Lyddon, PhD
Professor Director
University of Southern
 Mississippi
Hattiesburg, MS

Michael P. Maniacci, PsyD
Private Practice
Chicago, IL

Robert A. Neimeyer, PhD
Professor of Psychology
University of Memphis
Memphis, TN

Bernard H. Shulman, MD
Diamondhead Headache Clinic
Chicago, IL

Len Sperry, MD, PhD
Adjunct Professor
Barry University
MS Program in Health Services
 Administration
Miami Shores, FL

June Urschel, doctoral student
Adler School of Professional
 Psychology
Chicago, IL

Foreword

Perhaps one of Alfred Adler's most important contributions is his influence on other therapeutic orientations. Many of his basic ideas have found their way into other psychological schools, such as family systems approaches, Gestalt therapy, social learning theory, reality therapy, rational emotive behavioral therapy, cognitive therapy, person-centered therapy, and existential therapy. In some important respects, Adler seems to have paved the way for current developments in both cognitive and constructivist therapies. Both Adlerian theory and cognitive-behavioral therapy have many common precepts, and therapeutic efficacy can result from integrating the key concepts and techniques from both approaches. A study of contemporary counseling theories reveals that many of Adler's notions have reappeared in these modern approaches, with different nomenclature, and often without giving Adler the credit that is due him. Thus, in many respects, the postmodern approaches (social constructionism, solution-focused brief therapy and narrative therapy) resemble Adlerian theory and practice.

This book is more than a discourse on the contributions of Alfred Adler to the evolution of many of the contemporary approaches to counseling and psychotherapy. The book highlights ways in which Adlerian therapy, cognitive-behavioral therapies, and postmodern approaches share some common ground. Readers who want a further understanding of the similarities and differences of these therapy approaches will likely find the chapters in this book useful. The ideas presented here by the various authors point the way to developing an integrative approach to clinical practice. These various theoretical perspectives should not necessarily be viewed as inherently oppositional. Rather, possibly one may creatively reflect on the ways that therapeutic practice can be enhanced by selecting some of the key concepts and the specific techniques associated with each of the theories discussed in this volume.

Gerald Corey, EdD, ABPP
Professor Emeritus of Human Services
California State University, Fullerton

Acknowledgments

I say a sincere "thank you" to each of the authors for their contributions. I greatly appreciate your efforts—individually and collectively—toward completion of this project.

I also express my appreciation to Amanda O'Kelly for her assistance and attention to detail.

Last, but not least, I express my genuine gratitude and appreciation to the folks at Springer Publishing who were so helpful in bringing this project to fruition.

1

An Introduction to the Dialogue

Richard E. Watts

> "Alfred Adler, more than even Freud, is probably the true father of modern psychotherapy."
> —Albert Ellis

Over the past 20 years or so, there has been increasing interest in integration among psychotherapy theorists and practitioners. Historically, allegiance to specific theories or systems of psychotherapy was emphasized, and even expected, by particular theoretical schools or associations. However, the current zeitgeist emphasizes common ground and convergent themes. In fact, several journals focusing on integration have appeared in recent decades (Dinkmeyer & Sperry, 2000).

One may ask, "Why include Adler's theory in a book on psychotherapy integration?" Some may believe that Adlerian theory/therapy, having originated in the first half of the twentieth century, is not relevant to dialogues on contemporary psychotherapy integration. I believe a careful reading of this book will dispel that notion.

The quote by Ellis (1970), which begins this chapter, is indicative of the prophetic vision and significant influence of Alfred Adler regarding contemporary approaches to counseling and psychotherapy. Many consider Adler's influence on the development of other theories as his most important contribution to the field of counseling and psychotherapy (Corey, 1996). Adler's influence has been acknowledged and/or his vision traced to neo-Freudian approaches (e.g., Ansbacher & Ansbacher, 1979; Ellenberger, 1970), existential therapy (e.g., Frankl, 1963, 1970; May, 1970, 1989), person-centered therapy (e.g., Ansbacher, 1990; Watts, 1998), rational-emotive therapy (e.g., Dryden & Ellis, 1987; Ellis, 1970, 1973, 1989), cognitive therapy (e.g., Beck, 1976; Beck & Weishaar, 1989; Dowd & Kelly, 1980; Freeman, 1981, 1993; Freeman & Urschel, 1997; Raimy, 1975; Sperry, 1997), reality therapy (e.g., Glasser, 1984; Whitehouse, 1984; Wubbolding, 1993), family systems approaches (e.g., Broderick & Schrader, 1991; Carich & Willingham, 1987; Kern, Hawes, & Christensen, 1989; Nichols & Schwartz, 1995; Sherman, 1999; Sherman & Dinkmeyer, 1987), and constructivist and social constructionist perspectives (Carlson & Sperry, 1998; Disque & Bitter, 1998; Jones, 1995; Jones & Lyddon, 1997; LaFountain & Garner, 1998, 2002; Mahoney, 2002a, 2002b; Master, 1991; Schneider & Stone, 1998; Scott, Kelly, & Tolbert, 1995; Shulman & Watts, 1997; Watts, 1999, 2002; Watts & Critelli, 1997; Watts & Pietrzak, 2000).

Furthermore, the Adlerian approach is congruent with contemporary practice of psychotherapy. According to research by Prochaska and Norcross (2003), the current and near-future practice of psychotherapy will have the following characteristics: psychoeducational, present-oriented, and brief or time-limited approaches will be the norm; and integrative, eclectic, cognitive, and systemic theoretical orientations will be most utilized. Prochaska and Norcross's description appears to be consistent with the continuing demands of managed care and also appears to be supported by recent outcome research literature (Friedman, 1997; Hoyt, 1995; Hubble, Duncan, & Miller, 1999; Johnson, 1997; Miller, Hubble, & Duncan, 1996; Sauber, 1997; Sexton, Whiston, Bleuer, & Walz, 1999).

Persons familiar with the Adlerian approach will readily recognize the similarity between Prochaska and Norcross's (2003) description of the current/near-future field of psychotherapy and the contemporary practice of Adlerian therapy. Adlerian psychotherapy is a psychoeducational, present/future-oriented, and brief or time-limited approach. It is both integrative and eclectic, and combines cognitive and systemic perspectives. Consequently, Adlerian therapy solidly resonates with constructivist and social constructionist approaches to counseling and psychotherapy (Watts, 1999, 2000, 2002; Watts & Critelli, 1997; Watts & Pietrzak, 2000).

In 1997, I was guest editor for a special issue of the *Journal of Cognitive Psychotherapy* on the topic of "Adlerian and Cognitive Therapies." This volume is an extension and expansion of that initial effort. Four of the chapters have been significantly revised and updated, and two chapters are completely new contributions.[1]

Part 1 includes chapters by Adlerian and constructivist authors. In chapter 2, Richard E. Watts and Bernard H. Shulman discuss common ground and integrative potentialities between Adlerian and constructivist psychotherapies, from an Adlerian perspective. Chapter 3, by John V. Jones and William J. Lyddon, is a constructivist consideration of common ground and integration.

Part 2 includes chapters by Adlerian and cognitive therapy authors. Chapter 4, by Len Sperry, offers an Adlerian perspective on similarities between the two approaches and how each may benefit from careful study of the other. In chapter 5, Arthur Freeman and June Urschel provide insights, from a cognitive therapy perspective, regarding similarities and potential for mutual edification.

Part 3 provides responses to the four previous chapters by a cognitive therapy author, an Adlerian, and a constructivist. Rather than following the format of parts 1 and 2, the order of the chapters for part 3 was selected by alphabetical order of the authors' last names. E. Thomas Dowd, Michael P. Maniacci, and Robert A. Neimeyer provide thoughtful and occasionally pointed comments regarding the potentiality and viability of integration between Adlerian and cognitive and constructivist approaches.

Alfred Adler died in 1937, having created a personality theory and approach to counseling and psychotherapy so far ahead of his time that many contemporary approaches, particularly cognitive and constructivist perspectives, have embraced conclusions that clearly parallel many of Adler's fundamental ideas. Adler's ideas were out of step with the dominant metaphors of his time, and, consequently, his theory was discounted, even though many of his ideas have reappeared in subsequent theories of counseling and psychotherapy (Watts, 1999).

Many students, educators, and practitioners may view the Adlerian approach as an antiquated model, that is, one having limited utility in the contemporary integrative zeitgeist. In answer to the question, "Is Adlerian theory/therapy relevant for today's integrative discussion?" the diverse authors in this book demonstrate that the Adlerian approach soundly resonates with contemporary cognitive and constructivist thera-

---

[1] Although there are several editorial changes, chapter 5 by Freeman and Urschel has not been revised.

pies, and is indeed a relevant voice for inclusion in contemporary dialogues regarding integration.

REFERENCES

Ansbacher, H. L. (1990). Alfred Adler's influence on the three leading cofounders of humanistic psychology. *Journal of Humanistic Psychology, 30,* 45-53.

Ansbacher, H. L., & Ansbacher, R. R. (Eds.). (1979). *Superiority and social interest: A collection of Adler's later writings* (3rd ed.). New York: Norton.

Beck, A. T. (1976). *Cognitive therapy and the emotional disorders.* New York: Meridian.

Beck, A. T., & Weishaar, M. E. (1989). Cognitive therapy. In R. J. Corsini & D. Wedding (Eds.), *Current psychotherapies* (4th ed., pp. 285-322). Itasca, IL: Peacock.

Broderick, C. B., & Schraeder, S. S. (1991). The history of professional marriage and family therapy. In A. S. Gurman & D. P. Kniskern (Eds.), *Handbook of family therapy: Vol. II* (pp. 3-40). New York: Brunner/Mazel.

Carich, M. S., & Willingham, W. (1987). The roots of family systems theory in Individual Psychology. *Individual Psychology, 43,* 71-78.

Carlson, J., & Sperry, L. (1998). Adlerian psychotherapy as a constructivist psychotherapy. In M. F. Hoyt (Ed.), *The handbook of constructive therapies: Innovative approaches from leading practitioners* (pp. 68-82). San Francisco: Jossey-Bass.

Corey, G. (1996). *Theory and practice of counseling and psychotherapy* (5th ed.). Pacific Grove, CA: Brooks/Cole.

Dinkmeyer, D., Jr., & Sperry, L. (2000). *Counseling and psychotherapy: An integrated, Individual Psychology approach* (3rd ed.). Upper Saddle River, NJ: Merrill/Prentice Hall.

Disque, J. G., & Bitter, J. R. (1998). Integrating narrative therapy with Adlerian lifestyle assessment: A case study. *Journal of Individual Psychology, 54,* 431-450.

Dowd, E. T., & Kelly, F. D. (1980). Adlerian psychology and cognitive-behavior therapy: Convergences. *Journal of Individual Psychology, 36,* 119-135.

Dryden, W., & Ellis, A. (1987). Rational-emotive therapy. In W. Dryden & W. Golden (Eds.), *Cognitive-behavioural approaches to psychotherapy* (pp. 128-168). New York: Hemisphere.

Ellenberger, H. F. (1970). *The discovery of the unconscious.* New York: Basic Books.

Ellis, A. (1970). Humanism, values, rationality. *Journal of Individual Psychology, 26,* 11.

Ellis, A. (1973). *Humanistic psychotherapy.* New York: McGraw-Hill.

Ellis, A. (1989). Rational-emotive therapy. In R. J. Corsini & D. Wedding (Eds.), *Current psychotherapies* (4th ed., pp. 197-238). Itasca, IL: Peacock.

Frankl, V. E. (1963). *Man's search for meaning.* New York: Washington Square Press.

Frankl, V. E. (1970). Fore-runner of existential psychiatry. *Journal of Individual Psychology, 26,* 38.

Freeman, A. (1981). Dreams and images in cognitive therapy. In G. Emery & R. C. Bedrosian (Eds.), *New directions in cognitive therapy: A casebook* (pp. 224-238). New York: Guilford.

Freeman, A. (1993). Foreword. In L. Sperry & J. Carlson (Eds.), *Psychopathology and psychotherapy* (pp. iii-vi). Muncie, IN: Accelerated Development.

Freeman, A., & Urschel, J. (1997). Individual Psychology and cognitive-behavioral therapy: A cognitive therapy perspective. *Journal of Cognitive Psychotherapy, 11,* 165–179.
Friedman, S. (1997). *Time-effective psychotherapy.* Boston: Allyn & Bacon.
Glasser, W. (1984). Reality therapy. In R. J. Corsini (Ed.), *Current psychotherapies* (3rd ed., pp. 320–353). Itasca, IL: Peacock.
Hoyt, M. F. (1995). *Brief therapy and managed care.* San Francisco, CA: Jossey-Bass.
Hubble, M. A., Duncan, B. L., & Miller, S. D. (Eds.). (1999). *The heart and soul of change: What works in therapy.* Washington, DC: American Psychological Association.
Johnson, S. L. (1997). *Therapist's guide to clinical intervention: The 1-2-3s of treatment planning.* San Diego, CA: Academic Press.
Jones, J. V. (1995). Constructivism and Individual Psychology: Common ground for dialogue. *Individual Psychology, 51,* 231–243.
Jones, J. V., & Lyddon, W. J. (1997). Adlerian and constructivist psychotherapies: An constructivist perspective. *Journal of Cognitive Psychotherapy, 11,* 195–210.
Kern, R. M., Hawes, E. C., & Christensen, O. C. (1989). *Couples therapy: An Adlerian perspective.* Minneapolis: Educational Media Corporation.
LaFountain, R. M., & Garner, N. (1998). *A school with solutions: Implementing a solution-focused/Adlerian-based comprehensive schools counseling program.* Alexandria, VA: American School Counselor Association.
Mahoney, M. J. (2002a). Constructivism and positive psychology. In C. R. Snyder & S. J. Lopez (Eds.), *Handbook of positive psychology* (pp. 745–750). New York: Oxford University Press.
Mahoney, M. J. (2002b, July). *Constructive life counseling.* Workshop presented at the North American Personal Construct Network Conference, Vancouver, BC.
Master, S. B. (1991). Constructivism and the creative power of the self. *Individual Psychology, 47,* 447–455.
May, R. (1970). Myth and guiding fiction. *Journal of Individual Psychology, 26,* 39.
May, R. (1989). *The art of counseling* (Rev. ed.). New York: Gardner.
Miller, S. D., Hubble, M. A., & Duncan, B. L. (1996). *Handbook of solution-focused brief therapy.* San Francisco: Jossey-Bass.
Nichols, M. P., & Schwartz, R. C. (1995). *Family therapy: Concepts and methods* (3rd ed.). Boston: Allyn & Bacon.
Prochaska, J. O., & Norcross, J. C. (2003). *Systems of psychotherapy: A transtheoretical approach* (5th ed.). Pacific Grove, CA: Brooks/Cole.
Raimy, V. (1975). *Misunderstandings of the self.* New York: Jossey-Bass.
Sauber, S. R. (Ed.). (1997). *Managed mental health care: Major diagnostic and treatment approaches.* Bristol, PA: Brunner/Mazel.
Schneider, M. F., & Stone, M. (Guest Eds.). (1998). Narrative therapy and Adlerian psychology [Special issue]. *Journal of Individual Psychology, 54*(4).
Scott, C. N., Kelly, F. D., & Tolbert, B. L. (1995). Realism, constructivism, and the Individual Psychology of Alfred Adler. *Individual Psychology, 51,* 4–20.
Sexton, T. L., Whiston, S. C., Bleuer, J. C., & Walz, G. R. (1997). *Integrating outcome research into counseling practice and training.* Alexandria, VA: American Counseling Association.

Sherman, R. (1999). Family therapy: The art of integration. In R. E. Watts & J. Carlson (Eds.), *Interventions and strategies in counseling and psychotherapy* (pp. 101–134). Philadelphia: Accelerated Development/Taylor & Francis.

Sherman, R., & Dinkmeyer, D. (1987). *Systems of family therapy: An Adlerian integration.* New York: Brunner/Mazel.

Shulman, B. H., & Watts, R. E. (1997). Adlerian and constructivist psychotherapies: An Adlerian perspective. *Journal of Cognitive Psychotherapy, 11,* 181–193.

Sperry, L. (1997). Adlerian psychotherapy and cognitive therapy: An Adlerian perspective. *Journal of Cognitive Psychotherapy, 11,* 157–164.

Watts, R. E. (1998). The remarkable similarity between Rogers's core conditions and Adler's social interest. *Journal of Individual Psychology, 54,* 4–9.

Watts, R. E. (1999). The vision of Adler: An introduction. In R. E. Watts & J. Carlson (Eds.), *Interventions and strategies in counseling and psychotherapy* (pp. 1–13). Philadelphia: Accelerated Development/Taylor & Francis.

Watts, R. E. (2000). Entering the new millennium: Is Individual Psychology still relevant? *Journal of Individual Psychology, 56,* 21–30.

Watts, R. E. (2002, July). *Adlerian theory/therapy as a precursory exemplar of relational constructivism.* Paper presented at the North American Personal Construct Network Conference, Vancouver, BC.

Watts, R. E., & Critelli, J. W. (1997). Roots of contemporary cognitive theories in the Individual Psychology of Alfred Adler. *Journal of Cognitive Psychotherapy, 11,* 147–156.

Watts, R. E., & Pietrzak, D. (2000). Adlerian "encouragement" and the therapeutic process of solution-focused brief therapy. *Journal of Counseling and Development, 78,* 442–447.

Whitehouse, D. (1984). Adlerian antecedents to reality therapy and control theory. *Journal of Reality Therapy, 3,* 10–14.

Wubbolding, R. E. (1993). Reality therapy with children. In T. R. Kratochwill & R. J. Morris (Eds.), *Handbook of psychotherapy with children and adolescents* (pp. 288–219). Boston: Allyn & Bacon.

Part 1
Adlerian and Constructivist Psychotherapies

2

Integrating Adlerian and Constructive Therapies: An Adlerian Perspective

Richard E. Watts and Bernard H. Shulman

Corey (1996) stated that one of Adler's most important contributions to the field of counseling and psychotherapy was his influence on other systems. Given the recent epistemological shift in counseling toward a constructive perspective, it is not surprising to find that many ideas originally presented in the precursory postmodern theory of Alfred Adler have reappeared in contemporary counseling approaches, although often couched in different nomenclature and without acknowledgment of Adler's contribution. This appears to be particularly true relative to contemporary constructive approaches (Watts, 1999; Watts & Pietrzak, 2000).

The relationship between three popular postmodern/constructive approaches—constructivist therapy, solution-focused brief therapy, narrative therapy—and Adlerian psychology/psychotherapy is addressed to varying degrees in the literature, and a substantial number of common elements are identified. Adlerian and constructivist theories both affirm that humans are creative agents in the construction of their own personalities, and in the subsequent perceptions and interpretations of themselves, others, and the world (Carlson & Sperry, 1998; Jones, 1995; Master, 1991; Scott, Kelly, & Tolbert, 1995; Watts, 1999; Watts & Critelli, 1997). A wealth of common ground between Adlerian and solution-focused approaches is discussed in recent literature (LaFountain, 1996; LaFountain & Garner, 1998; Watts, 1999; Watts & Pietrzak,

2000). For example, Watts and Pietrzak (2000) identified a striking resemblance between the assumptions and characteristics of *encouragement*, as used in Adlerian therapy, and the therapeutic process of solution-focused brief therapy. Finally, a recent special issue of the *Journal of Individual Psychology* (Schneider & Stone, 1998), entitled "Narrative Therapy and Adlerian Psychology," identifies substantial common ground between the two approaches. For example, narrative and Adlerian approaches "resonate on the issue of social constructionism" (p. 414), and they share common therapeutic methods, albeit with different nomenclature.

As Dinkmeyer and Sperry (2000) note, "there is increasing interest in emphasizing the commonalities and converging themes among psychotherapy systems" (p. 9), and psychotherapy integration is the prevalent focus among many psychotherapy theorists, researchers, and practitioners. Given the noteworthy similarities between Adlerian theory/therapy and constructive approaches, we believe that an Adlerian–constructive integration would be a fruitful endeavor. To that end, the twofold purpose of this chapter is to (1) briefly explicate some of the many areas of common ground between Adlerian and constructive approaches, and (2) offer some reflections regarding areas for mutual edification and integration.

AREAS OF COMMON GROUND

According to Neimeyer (1995a), constructivists are joined by "their commitment to a common epistemology, or theory of knowledge" (p. 3) and "constructivism may also be distinguished by its operative assumptions about the nature of personal knowledge and its social embeddedness" (p. 5). Mahoney (1995b) notes that constructivism is essentially "a family of theories and therapies that emphasize at least three interrelated principles of human experience" (p. 44). These three central features of constructive metatheory include:

> (a) humans are proactive (and not passively reactive) participants in their own experience—that is, in all perception, memory and knowing; (b) the vast majority of ordering processes organizing human lives operate at tacit (un- or super-conscious) levels of awareness; and (c) human experience and personal psychological development reflect the ongoing operation of individualized, self-organizing processes that tend to favor the maintenance (over the modification) of experiential patterns. Although uniquely individ-

ual, these organizing processes always reflect and influence social systems. (pp. 44–45)

Neimeyer and Mahoney mention four areas that appear similar to fundamental tenets of Individual Psychology/Adlerian psychotherapy: philosophical roots, human agency, knowledge structures, and social embeddedness. In addition, Hoyt (1994) noted that, although the constructive approaches certainly have their differences, they share the following clinical-practical characteristics: They place strong emphasis on developing a strong, respectful therapeutic alliance; they emphasize strengths and resources; and they are optimistic and future-oriented. Again, the characteristics mentioned by Hoyt clearly resonate with Adlerian clinical practices. Thus, the theoretical characteristics mentioned by Neimeyer and Mahoney, in addition to a brief discussion of clinical issues, including those mentioned by Hoyt, serve as an outline for the common ground/integrative discussion.

Philosophical Roots

Adlerian and constructive theories clearly share common ground concerning their philosophical roots. In discussing the epistemology of constructivism, Neimeyer (1995b) notes:

> Every significant stream of thought has many tributaries. In the case of constructivism, these include wellsprings of philosophical inspiration for constructivism that can be traced back to Vico, Kant, and Vaihinger (Mahoney, 1988)—each of whom emphasized the proactive, form-giving, or fictional character of human mentation and its role in configuring the very "realities" to which we respond. (p. 11)

Like constructivism, the epistemological roots of Adlerian theory are mostly found in the critical philosophy of Immanuel Kant and the "as if" philosophy of Hans Vaihinger (Ansbacher & Ansbacher, 1956; Ellenberger, 1970; Shulman, 1985; Watts, 1999). In fact, Shulman (1985) states that Vaihinger was the key to Adler's casting of his theory in cognitive terms. Jones (1995) and Mahoney (1991), both constructivists, have acknowledged Kant and Vaihinger as common precursors for both Adler and constructivism. Both Kant and Vaihinger emphasized the proactive, form-giving, and fictional character of human cognition and its role in constructing the "realities" we know and to which we respond.

Adlerian theory asserts that humans construct, manufacture, or narratize ways of looking and experiencing the world, then take these *fictions* for truth (Ansbacher & Ansbacher, 1956; Ellenberger, 1970; Master, 1991; Watts, 1999).

In addition, Adler acknowledged the influence of Karl Marx and Friedrich Nietzsche on his theory (Ansbacher, 1983; Ansbacher & Ansbacher, 1956, 1979; Ellenberger, 1970). From Marx and Nietzsche, Adler gleaned ideas such as the socially embedded and fictional nature of human knowledge, the abilities and creativity of human beings, the necessity of egalitarian relationships and equal rights for all persons, and the socially useful and socially useless political and power issues involved in human relationships. Social constructionist therapies, via the writings of poststructural/postmodern theorists such as Derrida and Foucault, also have roots in the philosophies of Marx and Nietzsche (Gergen, 1994, 1999; Hoyt, 1996, 1998; Neimeyer & Raskin, 2000; White & Epston, 1990). Consequently, the ideas Adler gleaned from Marx and Nietzsche are among the prevalent themes discussed in social constructionist therapies.

Human Agency

The common ground between Adlerians and constructivists regarding human agency is noteworthy. According to Mahoney (1988, 1991, 1995a), constructivist theory espouses a proactive (versus reactive and representational) view of cognition and organism.

> What might well be considered the cardinal feature of constructivism is its assertion that *human knowing* is active, anticipatory, and literally 'constructive' (form-giving).... In one sense, then, constructivism argues that humans are literal co-creators of the 'realities' to which they respond. (Mahoney, Miller, & Arciero, 1995, p. 104)

This description of active, creative behavior in the organism sounds like what Adler called the *creative power of the self* or the *creative self*. In discussing human agency, Adler stated:

> Do not forget the most important fact that not heredity and not environment are determining factors. Both are giving only the frame and the influences which are answered by the individual in regard to his styled creative power (p. xxiv).... The individual is both the picture and the artist. He is the artist of his own personality. (Ansbacher & Ansbacher, 1956, p. 177)

Because of this creative power, humans function like actors writing their own scripts, directing their own actions, and forming their own personalities (Shulman, 1985).

> Human beings live in the realm of *meanings*. We do not experience things in the abstract; we always experience them in human terms. Even at its source our experience is qualified by our human perspective. . . . Anyone who tried to consider circumstances, to the exclusion of meanings, would be very unfortunate: he would isolate himself from others and his actions would be useless to himself or to anyone else; in a word, they would be meaningless. But no human being can escape meanings. We experience reality only through the meaning we ascribe to it: not as a thing in itself, but as something interpreted. (Adler, 1931/1992, p. 15)

According to Carlson and Sperry (1998), the realization that individuals coconstruct the reality in which they live, and are also able to "question, deconstruct, or reconstruct reality for themselves," is a fundamental tenet "not only of Adlerian psychotherapy but also of other constructivist psychotherapies" (p. 68).

Neimeyer and Mahoney (1995) noted that Maturana and Varela (1980) introduced a word into biology and other fields that describes the proactive, creative, and participatory nature of organisms described by constructivism: *autopoiesis*. This Greek word literally means "self" (auto) and "creative power or construction" (poiesis) (Neimeyer & Mahoney, 1995, p. 401). The nomenclature is essentially identical to Adler's creative power (or construction) of the self.

Knowledge Structures

There is much common ground between Adlerian and constructive theories on the subject of knowledge structures. In this section, we address (1) general descriptions of knowledge structures, (2) knowledge structures and unconscious processes, and (3) the unity of knowledge structures and resultant selective attention.

General Descriptions

As Disque and Bitter (1998) note, we live "storied" lives.

> As humans, we not only experience life directly through our senses, but we also transform it in an effort to make meaning out of what we experience.

We live constantly with other human beings, and as such, we frame all that we do in the context of social relationships. The ordering of the meaning we experience in our lives with others most often takes the form of a story or narrative about who we are; who others are; what we are worth to ourselves, others, and the world; and what conclusions, convictions, and ethical codes will guide us. . . . Adler was one of the first to recognize this process in human development. He called the ordering of our experiences into a teleological narrative our lifestyle, our unique way of being, of coping, and of moving through (and approaching the tasks of life). (p. 431)

According to most constructivists, the self constitutes an organized system or "meaning unit" (G. Neimeyer, 1995, p. 116) and has been variously referred to as "personal construct systems" (Kelly, 1955), "personal meaning organizations" (Guidano, 1991), "deep structures" (Guidano & Liotti, 1983, 1985), and "core ordering processes" (Mahoney, 1991). According to G. Neimeyer (1995), "These interconnected networks of meaning are taken to constitute the individual" (p. 116). Guidano and Liotti (1985) state that "knowledge appears to be a progressive hierarchic construction of models of reality where, step-by-step, the furniture of experience is moulded (sic) inside knowledge structures by the ordering activity carried out by the knowing subject" (p. 102). Cognition, they go on to say, is "the emergent result of the ongoing match between incoming information and contextual schemata" (p. 104). Thus, what we know is influenced by the frames through which we view events. Everything we know depends on how we interpret and assign meanings (Guidano, 1995a, 1995b; Neimeyer, 1995b). Social constructionists disdain the structural language used by cognitive constructivists, and the individualist implications thereof. They instead use literary metaphors like *narratives* or *stories*. Regardless of the language used by cognitive constructivists or social constructionists, both are nevertheless addressing how persons give—or construct—meaning to their experiences.

The above descriptions of knowledge structures, as "personal construct systems," "personal meaning organizations," "core ordering processes," "narratives," or "stories," are reminiscent of Adler's *style of life* or *lifestyle,* the superordinate rule for apprehending and responding to events and pressures. Mahoney (1988) acknowledged the similarity:

> Although the presence of organization in human experience may not be controversial, the nature and power of that organization take one into realms of less consensus. Few psychologists would challenge the notion that humans develop individually patterned lifestyles, for example, but many would hesitate

to embrace the concept of *lifestyle* as it was originally intended by Alfred Adler. Drawing on his familiarity with Vaihinger's philosophy of fictions, Adler viewed the lifestyle as an abstract organizing principle or construct that formatively influenced the contents and process of experience. (p. 7)

From the beginning, Adler cultivated a concept of a "psychological superstructure which organized and guided the mental life of the individual" (Stepansky, 1983). The psychological superstructure is a master plan or cognitive blueprint for coping with the tasks and challenges of life and is called the *lifestyle*. The lifestyle, unique to each individual, is, in Kelly's (1955) language, a *personal construct system*, containing *core constructs*. It is created by the person, begins as a rule of thumb for action in the world, and becomes progressively refined. Shulman (1973) and Shulman and Mosak (1988) have described the functions of the lifestyle: It organizes and simplifies coping with the world, by assigning rules and values; it selects, predicts, anticipates; its perceptions are guided by its own "private logic"; it selects what information it allows to enter, what it will attend to, what affects will be aroused, and what its response will be. According to Shulman (1985), lifestyle contains certain key elements. These include "a set of constructs about the self, the world, and the relationship between the two; a construct about what the relationship should be; an image of the ideal self; and a plan of action" (p. 246). All of these elements are attitudes, values, and meanings that the individual has creatively constructed within a socially embedded context.

Recent neurobiological research indicates that one of the brain's primary functions is to create a model of the world, an internal blueprint or roadmap. This model is established early in life and becomes reality, serves as a guide for subsequent life experiences, and selectively attends to (through modification or rejection) only that incoming data that fits with its program (Parry & Doan, 1994). The brain's function of creating an internal blueprint or roadmap is fundamentally similar to both constructive perspectives and the Adlerian idea of the relationally cocreated style of life.

Knowledge Structures and Unconscious Processes

According to constructivism, the knowledge structures, or core ordering processes, by which humans organize and construct meaning for reality, are mostly unconscious.

> From a constructivist perspective, tacit (unconscious) processes of mental activity are deep structure ordering rules that organize ongoing experience and anticipate imminent experience. This means that abstract tacit processes operate passively in our experience, and yet, as the words *abstract* and *tacit* imply, their operations are well beyond our conscious awareness. (Guidano, 1995a, p. 92)

The above quote is similar to the Adlerian position concerning an individual's lifestyle. Humans are not typically aware of the convictions that guide their lives. The style of life is the blueprint or map for coping with experience, but it nevertheless remains mostly out of one's awareness—Adler's process understanding of unconscious. Thus, both the construction of the individual's unique style of life and the goals and core convictions contained therein are also essentially unconscious (Allen, 1971; Mosak, 1979; Shulman, 1985). As Mosak (1995) explains, "Although the life-style is the instrument for coping with experience, it is very largely nonconscious" (p. 63).

Unity of Knowledge Structures and Selective Attention

According to constructivist theory, knowledge structures of the human organism are unified in their processes and, therefore, selectively attend to those aspects of reality that confirm and support their maintenance.

> The search for consistency (maintenance processes) is the basic procedure for structuring and stabilizing available levels of self-identity and self-awareness.... Change processes derive from attempts to convert emergent core schemata into beliefs and thought procedures and are regulated and modeled, step by step, by maintenance processes aimed at preserving the functional continuity and the sense of oneness inherent in selfhood structures. (Guidano, 1995a, p. 97)

Adlerian theory sees the unity of personality and concomitant perceptual selectivity of the human organism in similar ways. According to Adlerian theory, "personality (lifestyle) is a *unity*, an organized and integrated whole" (Forgus & Shulman, 1979, p. 107). The lifestyle organizes and maintains the whole perceptual system of the individual, resulting in selective perceptual processing of all incoming information. Thus, the organism looks for information confirming the core convictions of the lifestyle, "selectively perceiving information from events so that it proves to itself what it already suspects" (Shulman, 1985, p. 246). The great majority of cognitive functions (e.g., memory, learning, expectancy, fantasy, symbol creation) are influenced by perceptual selectivity. "One result of the (lifestyle) is thus a private frame of reference by which the individual orients himself (or herself) and arranges his (or her) coping strategies in the world-as-perceived" (p. 247).

Social Embeddedness

The common ground between Adlerian and constructive theories regarding social embeddedness is especially striking. As mentioned earlier, Neimeyer (1995b) comments that one of the distinguishing marks of constructivism is its "operative assumptions about the structure of personal knowledge and its social embeddedness" (p. 15). Constructivists affirm that humans are undeniably social beings and that "any knowledge of oneself and the world is always dependent on and relative to knowledge of others" (Guidano, 1995b, p. 96). Constructivism attends to the dynamic interaction between the "organism and its milieu," paying particular attention to "social support systems, family and developmental history, cultural contexts, and ultimately the therapeutic relationship" (Mahoney, 1995a, p. 12). Concerning early family and developmental history, Guidano (1995b) affirms that constructivists find utility in John Bowlby's attachment theory.

> Within an intersubjective reality, attachment exerts an organizational role in the development of a sense of self both as subject and as object.... Through regularities drawn from caregivers' behaviors and affective messages, the infant can begin to construct basic feelings that are inseparable from early perceptions, actions, and memories. (p. 97)

The constructive view of social embeddedness echoes the position taken by Adler (Ansbacher & Ansbacher, 1956, 1979) and subsequent Adlerians. Adler noted that humans are socially embedded and cannot be understood apart from their social context. Manaster and Corsini (1982) state that the human personality or lifestyle "evolves from a biological being in a social context creating a sense of self in the world in which he (or she) acts" (p. 77). This social context of the child includes both the cultural values of the child's culture of origin and his or her experiences within his or her *family constellation,* Adler's phrase for the operative influences of the family structure, values, and dynamics (Shulman, 1985). Thus, "the child sees the world in general as paralleling his (or her) home environment and eventually the wider world on the basis of his (or her) initial perceptions" (Manaster & Corsini, 1982, p. 91).

Peluso, White, and Kern (2001) discuss the similarity between essential elements of attachment theory and Adlerian psychology: "The major areas of convergence between the two theories are that both include a coherent and stable view of self and the world, and both acknowledge the importance of social interaction for the expression of these patterns" (p. 4). As Peluso et al. indicate, the parallels between the development of attachment theory's *internal working model* and Adler's style of life are remarkable indeed. They note that the lifestyle, like the internal working model of self and others, is an internalized subjective creation based on relationships with early primary caregivers and family members, "therefore, both the internal working model of self and others, and the lifestyle are important because they have a lasting impact on an individual's work relationships, friendships, and selection of a partner" (p. 12).

> The cardinal tenet of Adler's theory, *social interest,* is obviously a social-contextual one. The tendency of human beings to form attachments (social feelings) was considered by Adler to be a fact of life. The striving of the human is always in some way connected with human bonding. Social interest is the expression of this tendency in a way that promotes human welfare. Some aspects of social interest are innate as in the infant's tendency to bond with its mother. However, social interest is a potential that must be developed through training in cooperation with productive endeavor. (Shulman, 1985, p. 248)

The development of the attachment motive in attachment theory appears to parallel the development of Adler's social interest. Both are innate, both have to be developed in interaction with primary caregivers, and the degree to which both are present in an individual's life impacts the degree to which that person moves toward or against/away from fellow human beings (Ainsworth, 1964; Ansbacher & Ansbacher, 1979; Bowlby, 1982; Forgus & Shulman, 1979; Peluso et al., 2001). According to Mosak and Maniacci (1999):

> Constructionists believe that through early bonding interactions, individuals learn to encode and process information in such a way as to feel secure. This becomes the basis of later attempts to bond with others; hence, if early attachment was disturbed or in any significant way disordered, as adults, we may continue the inappropriate attempts at bonding in much the same manner as we did as children. In fact, most constructionists believe that

psychopathology is itself a disordered attempt at bonding. This is Adler's and Dreikurs' opinion as well. Adlerians believe that psychopathology is a discouraged attempt at belonging. (p. 169).

Peluso et al. (2001) also address the parallels between attachment styles and social interest. Adlerian psychology views social interest as the measure of mental health. Social interest, like attachment style, is developed from the earliest social relationships, primarily the family. Peluso et al. indicate that persons described as "securely attached," according to attachment theory, manifest behaviors descriptive of persons with elevated social interest. Conversely, persons with anxious or ambivalent attachment exhibit behaviors descriptive of lower levels of social interest. Thus, securely attached children with an elevated level of social interest are more likely to engage life optimistically and courageously. Thus, both attachment and social interest address the mental health of individuals. As Mosak (1995) notes: "If we regard ourselves as fellow human beings with fellow feeling (social interest), we are socially contributive people interested in the common welfare and, by Adler's pragmatic definition of *normality,* mentally healthy" (p. 53).

Therapy Issues

Hoyt (1994) states that, although the constructive approaches certainly have their differences, they share the following clinical-practical characteristics: They place strong emphasis on developing a respectful therapeutic relationship, they emphasize strengths and resources, and they are optimistic and future-oriented. Again, this statement by Hoyt is equally descriptive of Adlerian therapy. Given the aforementioned areas of common ground between Adlerians and constructive approaches, it is not surprising to find much common ground regarding the process of therapy. We found that Adlerians and constructive therapies share common beliefs about many clinical issues. For the sake of brevity, however, we address only four: perspective on maladjustment, client reluctance to change, the client–therapist relationship, and facilitating change.

Perspective on Maladjustment

Constructive descriptions of motivation for therapy parallel the Adlerian position. Both eschew the medical model perspective and embrace a nonpathological perspective. They both agree that clients are not sick (as in having a disease) and thus are not identified or labeled by their diagnoses (de Shazer, 1991; Disque & Bitter, 1998; Hoyt, 1994, 1996, 1998; Littrell, 1998; Manaster & Corsini, 1982; Mosak, 1995; Neimeyer & Raskin, 2000; Parry & Doan, 1994; Schneider & Stone, 1998; Walter & Peller, 1992; Watts, 1999; Watts & Pietrzak, 2000; White & Epston, 1990). According to Parry and Doan (1994):

> The experiences that bring individuals or families to therapy represent, in our view, a "wake up call"—a message that the stories that have formed them and shaped their emotional reactions have reached their limit. Although these stories made sense to children dependent upon adults, they are no longer adequate to help individuals handle present challenges effectively. It is now time for them to question the beliefs and assumptions that their stories have coded, in order to free themselves from the constraints upon capacities that maturity and responsibility have since made available to them. (p. 42)

Littrell (1998) states that clients present for counseling because they are demoralized or discouraged, not because they are sick and in need of a cure. Clients "lack hope. . . . One of our tasks as counselors is to assist in the process of restoring patterns of hope" (p. 63).

The constructive position on maladjustment soundly resonates with the Adlerian model. Adlerians agree that early existential decisions about self and the world—decisions made within and relative to the first sociological environment, the family—form the core convictions of a client's lifestyle or his or her "story of my life" (Adler, 1931/1992). Adlerians agree that many of the early formed convictions may have been useful for a child to belong to, and survive in, his or her early environment, but later prove to no longer be useful for productive living. In addition, a crucial goal of Adlerian therapy is to help clients challenge and modify or replace growth-inhibiting life themes with ones that are growth-enhancing. The ultimate goal is the development or enhancement of clients' social interest.

Because they do not see clients as sick, Adlerians are not about curing anything. Rather, in agreement with constructive approaches, therapy is "a process of encouragement" (Manaster & Corsini, 1982, p. 160). Dreikurs (1967) noted the essential necessity of encouragement in counseling. He stated that presenting problems are "based on discouragement" and, without "encouragement, without having faith in himself restored, (the client) cannot see the possibility of doing or functioning better" (p. 62). Adler once asked a client what he thought made the difference in his successful experience in therapy. The client replied: "That's quite simple. I had lost all courage to live. In our consultations I found it again" (Ansbacher & Ansbacher, 1956, p. 342).

Adlerians view clients as discouraged rather than sick, and they thus view client symptoms from a proactive rather than merely reactive perspective. According to Mosak and Maniacci (1999), symptoms are selected and chosen because they are perceived as facilitating movement toward a desired goal. In other words, symptoms are not merely reactions to situations, but rather attempted solutions.

Client Reluctance to Change

According to Mahoney et al. (1995), constructivists believe that the core ordering processes of human beings are less accessible and amenable to change. Furthermore, when these' core ordering processes are challenged or threatened in therapy, clients will manifest self-protective mechanisms, in order to preserve the integrity of their core meaning system (G. Neimeyer, 1995). According to Liotti, "A cognitive structure that attributes meaning and casual relationships to an important class of emotional experiences will be quite resistant to change if the individual does not develop alternative meaning structures" (quoted in G. Neimeyer, 1995, p. 116). G. Neimeyer (1995) comments that this self-protective view is common to many constructive approaches.

Adlerians also espouse a self-protective view of client reluctance to change. According to Shulman (1985), the core constructs of Adlerian theory's lifestyle are essentially unconscious and are also less accessible and amenable to change. When these core lifestyle convictions are challenged (in life or in therapy), the client often responds by use of compensation. According to Mosak (1995), the word *compensation* was used by Adler as an umbrella to cover all the problem-solving devices clients use to safeguard their self-esteem, reputation, and physical self. As in the constructivist perspective, Adlerians view client reluctance to change in terms of clients self-protecting or safeguarding their sense of self (Shulman, 1985).

Client–Therapist Relationship

The constructivist therapist, according to Neimeyer (1995b), "adopts an empathic, collaborative, respectful, and at times reverential, mode of relating to the client" (p. 18).

> Constructivists are wary of an exclusive dedication to technique, preferring instead to emphasize the critical role of therapeutic relationship in enabling and initiating human change. . . . For constructivists, psychotherapeutic technique occurs in relational contexts. For that reason, in most constructive therapies a premium is placed on forging an intimate therapeutic bond between the client and therapist. (G. Neimeyer, 1995, pp. 113–114)

G. Neimeyer (1995) notes that "constructivists regard the therapeutic relationship as a kind of home base, or emotional tether, for the client to use in his or her personal exploration" (p. 114). In further describing the therapeutic relationship, he states that constructivist therapies attempt to provide the client a kind of permissive acceptance, see the problem and the world through the client's eyes, and manifest an attitude that is more inquisitive, approving, and exploratory than it is disputational, disapproving, and demonstrative.

Watts and Pietrzak (2000) note that constructive therapies describe the client–counselor relationship using words such as "cooperative," "collaborative," "egalitarian," "mutual," "optimistic," "respectful," and "shared." In developing the relationship, constructive therapists focus on developing a strong therapeutic alliance, trusting the client, and exploring clients' competencies. Most of the basic skills used in building this relationship are not unique to constructive approaches. In addition, Littrell (1998) states, "Strategies and techniques are ineffectual if the facilitative conditions of warmth, genuineness, and empathy do not permeate the counseling process" (p. 8).

Of the many areas of common ground shared between Adlerian theory and constructive approaches, the view of the therapeutic relationship may well be the most similar. All the words used in the constructive therapy literature to describe the counselor–client relationship are also used in the Adlerian literature (e.g., Ansbacher & Ansbacher, 1956; Dreikurs, 1967; Dinkmeyer, Dinkmeyer, & Sperry, 1987; Mosak, 1979; Sweeney, 1998; Watts, 1999; Watts & Pietrzak, 2000). For Adlerians, a strong counselor–client relationship is usually developed when counselors model social interest. Watts (1998) noted that Adler's descriptions of therapist-modeled social interest look very similar to Carl Rogers's descriptions of the core facilitative conditions of client change: congruence, unconditional positive regard, and empathic understanding. Furthermore, Mosak (1979) discusses the counselor–client relationship in terms of "faith, hope, and love" (p. 63), that is, expressing faith in clients and helping them develop faith in themselves, instilling hope in clients, and helping clients experience a relationship with an individual who truly cares. The basic skills necessary to build the therapeutic

An Adlerian Perspective

alliance, as discussed in the Adlerian literature (e.g., Dinkmeyer, Dinkmeyer, et al., 1987; Mosak, 1979), are, in the main, the same ones mentioned in constructive therapy literature (e.g., DeJong & Berg, 1998; Littrell, 1998).

Adlerian therapy typically is viewed as consisting of four phases: relationship, analysis, insight, and reorientation (Mosak, 1995). The first and, for most Adlerians, most important stage is entitled *relationship*. The Adlerian approach is a relational psychology and psychotherapy. Because psychotherapy occurs in a relational context, Adlerian therapists focus on developing a respectful, collaborative, and egalitarian therapeutic alliance with clients. Therapeutic efficacy in other phases of Adlerian therapy is predicated upon the development and continuation of a strong therapeutic relationship (Watts, 1998, 2000; Watts & Pietrzak, 2000).

Facilitating Change

Constructive therapists seek to help clients change their behaviors and attitudes from a problem/failure focus to a focus on solutions/successes, and discover and/or develop latent assets, resources, and strengths that may have been overlooked as clients have focused primarily on problems and limitations (Watts & Pietrzak, 2000). According to O'Hanlon & Weiner-Davis (1989), counselors using this approach are trying to do three things:

1. Change the "doing" of the situation that is perceived as problematic. By helping clients change their present actions and interactions, they become free to "use other, atypical actions that are more likely to resolve their situations than repeating unsuccessful patterns" (p. 126).
2. Change the "viewing" of the situation that is perceived as problematic. Facilitating changes in clients' frames of reference, both in and out of counseling, may produce changes in behavior and/or elicit untapped strengths and abilities.
3. Evoke resources, solutions, and strengths to bring to the situation that is perceived as problematic. Reminding clients of their abilities, resources, and strengths may create changes in behaviors or perceptions.

Littrell (1998) adds:

As counselors we help clients find and/or create patterns of thoughts, feelings, actions, and meaning. We code these patterns with names like "resources" or "abilities" or "inner strengths." Some patterns we rediscover from clients' pasts; some are currently being used but clients have not yet recognized them as such. We can also cocreate new patterns that do not yet exist in clients' repertoire or we can modify current ones. (pp. 63–64)

Again, the similarity between constructive therapies and Adlerian therapy is remarkable. As stated earlier, Hoyt (1994) identified three clinical-practical characteristics that constructive approaches share. These characteristics essentially mirror what Adlerians have historically called *encouragement,* or the therapeutic modeling of social interest. For Adlerians, encouragement is both an attitude and a way of being with clients in therapy (Watts, 1999). According to Watts and Pietrzak (2000), Adler and subsequent Adlerians consider encouragement a crucial aspect of human growth and development. This is especially true in the field of counseling. Stressing the importance of encouragement in therapy, Adler stated: "Altogether, in every step of the treatment, we must not deviate from the path of encouragement" (Ansbacher & Ansbacher, 1956, p. 342). Dreikurs (1967) agreed: "What is most important in every treatment is encouragement" (p. 35). In addition, Dreikurs (1967) stated that therapeutic success was greatly dependent upon "(the therapist's) ability to provide encouragement" and failure generally occurred "due to the inability of the therapist to encourage" (pp. 12–13).

> Encouragement focuses on helping counselees become aware of their worth. By encouraging them, you help your counselees recognize their own strengths and assets, so they become aware of the power they have to make decisions and choices.... Encouragement focuses on beliefs and self-perceptions. It searches intensely for assets and processes feedback so the client will become of aware of her (or his) strengths. In a mistake-centered culture like ours, this approach violates norms by ignoring deficits and stressing assets. The counselor is concerned with changing the client's negative self concept and anticipations. (Dinkmeyer et al., 1987, p. 124)

Encouragement skills include demonstrating concern for clients through active listening and empathy; communicating respect for and confidence in clients, focusing on clients' strengths, assets, and resources; helping clients generate perceptual alternatives for discouraging fictional beliefs; focusing on efforts and progress, and helping clients see the humor in life experiences (Ansbacher & Ansbacher, 1956; Carlson & Slavik, 1997; Dinkmeyer, 1972; Dinkmeyer, Dinkmeyer, et al., 1987; Dinkmeyer & Losoncy, 1980; Dreikurs, 1967; Mosak, 1979; Mosak & Maniacci, 1998; Neuer, 1936; Sweeney, 1998; Watts, 1999; Watts & Pietrzak, 2000).

In agreement with constructive approaches, Adlerians are *technical eclectics* (Manaster & Corsini, 1982). As such, they use a variety of cognitive, behavioral, and experiential techniques to help clients create new patterns of behavior, develop more encouraging perceptions, and access resources and strengths (Adler, 1929; Dinkmeyer, 1972; Dinkmeyer, Dinkmeyer, et al., 1987; Dreikurs, 1967; Mosak, 1979; Sweeney, 1998; Watts, 1999). Thus, as part of the encouragement process, Adlerians help clients identify and combat discouraging cognitions; generate perceptual alternatives; focus on efforts, not merely outcomes; and emphasize assets, resources, and strengths (Ansbacher & Ansbacher, 1956; Dinkmeyer, 1972; Dinkmeyer, Dinkmeyer, et al., 1987; Dreikurs, 1967; Mosak, 1979; Watts & Pietrzak, 2000).

Even though Adlerian counseling is a technically eclectic approach, it does, nevertheless, have a number of techniques originally created by Adlerians, many of which look rather similar to techniques that are claimed as original by some constructive therapy authors. These include acting "as if," catching oneself, confrontation, the magic wand technique, prescribing the symptom (paradoxical intention), pushbutton, spitting in the soup, the question, task-setting, and the tentative hypothesis/interpretation (Dinkmeyer, Dinkmeyer, et al., 1987; Manaster & Corsini, 1982; Mosak, 1979, 1995; Sweeney, 1998). Additional sources for examining Adlerian techniques include Carlson and Slavik (1997), Mosak and Maniacci (1998), and Watts and Carlson (1999).

Contemporary therapists are expected to be integrative and eclectic. Adlerian therapy, like constructive approaches, is a very flexible approach that is highly integrative and technically eclectic. Adlerian therapy allows therapists to do whatever is in the best interest of clients, rather than forcing clients, and their unique situations, into one therapeutic framework. There is great value in a broad theoretical model like Adlerian therapy. As Bitter (1997) notes, a broad model "allows for growth and development from within as well as integration of useful interventions from other models" (p. 372). Regardless of one's theoretical orientation, however, the encouragement process is one of many aspects of Adlerian therapy that may be usefully integrated in a therapist's approach to counseling. The assumptions, characteristics, and methods of encouragement help to create an optimistic, empowering, and growth-enhancing environment for clients—a place where they feel "en-abled" rather than "dis-abled" (Watts & Pietrzak, 2000).

REFLECTIONS FOR EDIFICATION AND INTEGRATION

Although there are several important things that Adlerian and constructive theorists and practitioners can learn from the other, space permits the offering of only a few reflections.

Reflections for Adlerians

The Language of Constructivism

Adler always tried to use everyday language ("common sense"), because he wanted to reach the general public. That fact often led him to be misunderstood by the scientific community and to be accused of oversimplication. The lack of a more technical terminology often made it difficult to compare Adler to others, so later Adlerian authors found it necessary to look for ways of translating Adler into the language of contemporary theories. After having attempted this through behaviorism, interpersonal psychiatry, neo-Freudian theories, existentialism, Gestalt therapy, transactional analysis, object relations, and self-psychology, we must admit that we find the technical language of constructivism comfortable, because, in most respects, it is quite congruent with Adlerian theory. As Mahoney et al. (1995) commented: "Constructivism is . . . a complexly commonsensical approach" (p. 105). Thus, we believe the language of constructivism is more precise and its formulations will be useful to Adlerian psychology thinkers who continue to develop Adler's theory.

Structuralism and Functionalism

Jones (1995) mentions that Adlerians have hesitated to accept a structural point of view, because the notion of psychic structures has possible connotations or reminders of psychoanalytic id–ego–superego thinking. He may be correct, because Adlerians have insisted on maintaining an open-systems model and have tried to avoid any hard determinism. However, constructivists have demonstrated that one may embrace both structuralism and functionalism. Mahoney et al. (1995) state that *structuralism,* as it is used by many contemporary European psychologists, refers to "a conceptual and literary tradition associated with de Saussure, Jakobson, Levi-Strauss, Marx, Greimas, and Barthes" (p. 108). The authors affirmed that this tradition forms the literary firmament from which the revolutionary poststructuralist thinking of authors such as Lacan, Foucault, and Derrida emerged: "The difference between the two uses (of structuralism) is formidable and should be noted" (p. 108).

> Constructivist views of structure cover a wide range of intended means. Of particular importance to this discussion is the predominantly North American emphasis on *static ordering relationships*, which should be contrasted with the (contemporary) European tendency to view structure as *dynamic, developmental, and dialectical.* (p. 109)

Viewed from this perspective, constructivists state that functionalism and structuralism actually work together and claim that determinism is not a logical consequence of a structural position. "Because Adlerians want to eliminate dichotomies such as mind–body and conscious–unconscious, the constructivist's position on structuralism and functionalism, consistent with a holistic perspective, might serve as some fertile common ground between the two camps" (Jones, 1995, p. 235). For Adlerians willing to take this step, constructivism offers a useful conceptual set, the concept of structures of cognition, and deep and peripheral structures.

Research

There is not a large body of research literature in support of Adler's theory. Because of the numerous similarities between Adlerian and constructive theories, however, the burgeoning constructive research literature may offer added support and validation to Adlerian psychology and psychotherapy and serve as a catalyst for refinement and modification of the theory (e.g., Hubble, Duncan, & Miller, 1999).

Reflections for Constructivists

Integrative Constructivism

Lyddon (1995) states that a more integrative constructivist theory will include material, efficient, formal, and telic dimensions of human cognition. Adlerian theory presently contains all four dimensions. Through a thorough examination of Adlerian theory, constructivists may find ideas that have utility in the constructive movement toward integration.

For example, Adlerian theory is further developed in areas such as the concept of movement through the life span, in terms of goal-directed striving and the concept of striving with or without community feeling/social interest (*gemeinschaftsgefuhl*). Mosak and Maniacci (1999) note that the Adlerian theory and system has more to offer us than historical significance: "By learning the principles and applications of Adlerian psychology, it is *easier* to make the transition to contemporary clinical practice within other systems of thought" (p. 9).

Uncovering Core Constructs/Personal Narratives

Because constructive therapists, like Adlerians, hold such high regard for the influence of early life experiences on the construction of core constructs or personal narratives, they may find utility in how Adlerians go about uncovering these constructs/narratives through use of lifestyle analysis. Watts (1999) notes that the Adlerian use of lifestyle analysis, including use of early recollections, helps to, in constructive nomenclature, uncover the *hidden text* in the client's life story. This hidden text is reminiscent of core constructs or lifestyle themes in what Adler (1931/1992) called the client's "story of my life."

Specific ways of describing a lifestyle were in use by Adlerians early on, but were not published until later (Allen, 1971; Baruth & Eckstein, 1981; Eckstein, Baruth, & Mahrer, 1982; Gushurst, 1971; Powers & Griffith, 1987; Shulman, 1973; Shulman & Mosak, 1988). Shulman and Mosak's (1988) *Life Style Inventory,* for example, is a structured questionnaire addressing early childhood experiences and the structure and interrelations of the family of origin, and the earliest childhood recollections.

Beyond Individual Therapy

The Adlerian literature contains a wealth of information on couple and family therapy, relationship enrichment and parent education, group therapy, and public education. These topics have been addressed by Adlerians regularly in the Adlerian journal, the *Journal of Individual Psychology,* occasionally in mainstream counseling and psychotherapy journals, and in various books authored by Adlerians (e.g., Carlson & Dinkmeyer, 1999; Christensen, 1993; Dinkmeyer, 1971; Dinkmeyer & Carlson, 1984; Dinkmeyer & Dreikurs, 1963; Dinkmeyer, McKay, Dinkmeyer, et al., 1987; Dinkmeyer & Muro, 1971; Dinkmeyer & Sperry, 2000;

Dreikurs, 1968; Dreikurs & Soltz, 1964; Grunwald, 1971; Grunwald & McAbee, 1985; Kern, Hawes, & Christensen, 1989; Kottman, 1995; Mosak, 1971; Mosak & Maniacci, 1999; Sherman, 1999; Sherman & Dinkmeyer, 1987; Sweeney, 1998; Watts & Carlson, 1999). Given the theoretical compatibility between Adlerian and constructive approaches, constructive therapists may find value in examining the Adlerian literature on these topics.

Multicultural Considerations

With the increasing emphasis on multiculturalism, many counselors have been drawn to postmodern approaches, because of their focus on the social embeddedness of humans and, consequently, human knowledge. Adlerians and Adlerian theory addressed social equality issues and emphasized the social embeddedness of humans and human knowledge, long before multiculturalism became a focal issue in the profession (Watts, 1999; Watts & Pietrzak, 2000). Adler campaigned for the social equality of women, contributed much to the understanding of gender issues, spoke against the marginalization of minority groups, and specifically predicted the black power and women's liberation movements (Ansbacher & Ansbacher, 1978; Dreikurs, 1971; Hoffman, 1994; LaFountain & Mustaine, 1998; Mozdzierz, 1998). LaFountain and Mustaine (1998) note that Adlerian theory played an influential role in the historic *Brown v. Board of Education* decision of May 17, 1954.

> Kenneth B. Clark headed a team of social scientists who called on Adlerian theory to explain the need for equality in American society. Their argument against separate-but-equal schools swayed the highest court in its decision that ruled in favor of the plaintiffs. (p. 196)

One may ask, Is the Adlerian approach relevant for working with culturally diverse populations in contemporary society? Gerald Corey's invited commentary, included in a 1991 special issue of the *Journal of Mental Health Counseling* entitled "Macrostrategies in Mental Health Counseling," offers an affirmative reply:

> The basic assumptions of all these authors [Herr, Ivey, Rigazio-DiGilio, and Dinkmeyer] appear to rest on an Adlerian foundation that stresses prevention, policies that are growth producing, visions that inspire individuals to feel competent, the process of reaching out to others, and finding meaning and a sense of community in a social context.... From my vantage point, Adler's ideas are certainly compatible with many of the macrostrategies for future

delivery of services to culturally diverse populations. (quoted in Sweeney, 1998, pp. 33–34)

Furthermore, Arciniega and Newlon (1999), in a chapter entitled "Counseling and Psychotherapy: Multicultural Considerations," state that the contemporary counseling theory holding the greatest promise for addressing multicultural issues is Adlerian theory. They note that the characteristics and assumptions of Adlerian psychology are congruent with the cultural values of many minority racial and ethnic groups. In addition, Arciniega and Newlon affirm that the Adlerian therapeutic process is respectful of cultural diversity:

> Adlerian goals are not aimed at deciding for clients what they should change about themselves. Rather, the practitioner works in collaboration with clients and their family networks. This theory offers a pragmatic approach that is flexible and uses a range of action-oriented techniques to explore personal problems within their sociocultural context. It has the flexibility to deal both with the individual and the family, making it appropriate for racial and ethnic groups. (p. 451)

Religion and Spirituality

The field of counseling and psychotherapy has made a 180-degree turn, from a position of disdain and avoidance, to one beginning to appreciate the influence of spiritual issues on cognition, emotion, and, ultimately, behavior (Propst, 1996). According to Mahoney (1995b), "issues of value—good–bad, right–wrong, and sacred–profane" will become increasingly central in the future of psychotherapy, "with the dimensions of religiosity and spirituality taking on new meanings in psychological assessment" (p. 55).

The importance of attending to clients' spirituality in counseling and psychotherapy cannot be emphasized too strongly. One key value central to many clients is their personal spirituality. Without understanding their clients' spiritual perspective, therapists are "operating with a vital value system and possibly even a member of the family, God, left at home and ignored" (Grizzle, 1992, p. 139). Spirituality is a vital area for therapists to understand, because clients' spiritual beliefs typically provide the value system by which they view themselves, others, and the world. To ignore or discount clients' spirituality is to close one's eyes to a vital therapeutic factor.

Historically, most systems of psychology have had either a neutral or negative position toward religion and spirituality. Individual psychology and Adlerian therapy, however, have been more open than many other approaches concerning religious and spiritual issues. Constructive practitioners may find utility in the manner in which many Adlerians have comfortably engaged religious and spiritual matters. The topic is addressed regularly by authors in the *Journal of Individual Psychology* (e.g., Mansager, 2000).

According to Manaster and Corsini (1982), "the most common Adlerian position toward religion is positive, viewing God as the concept of perfection. . . . For Adler, religion was a manifestation of social interest" (p. 63). Mosak (1995) notes that "Adler's psychology has a religious tone. His placement of social interest at the pinnacle of his value theory is in the tradition of those religions that stress people's responsibility for each other" (p. 59). Mosak (1995) mentioned that, when Adler introduced the concepts of *value* and *meaning* into psychology via his 1931 book, *What Life Should Mean to You*, the concepts were unpopular at the time. The cardinal tenet of Adlerian theory is social interest, and Adler equated it with the mandate to "love one's neighbor as oneself" and the golden rule. Furthermore, Mosak identifies *spirituality* as one of the five major tasks of life: "Although Adler alluded to the *spiritual*, he never specifically named it. But each of us must deal with the problems of defining the nature of the universe, the existence and nature of God, and how to relate to these concepts" (p. 54).

CONCLUSION

How well do constructive approaches fit in with Adler's theory? They appear to fit very well indeed. After a close look, these different theories, using different nomenclature, appear to say very similar things. Contemporary therapies, especially constructive approaches, consistently express positions congruent with the Adlerian perspective. According to Watts (1999),

> Adler died in 1937 having created a personality theory and approach to therapy so far ahead of its time that contemporary "cutting-edge" theories and therapies are only now "discovering" many of Adler's fundamental conclusions, typically without reference to or acknowledgment of Adler. (p. 8)

Neimeyer (2000) suggests that an integrative bridge between cognitive constructivist and social constructionist perspectives might be usefully labeled *relational constructivism*. It appears to us that Adlerian theory and therapy could serve as that integrative bridge. As noted throughout this chapter, the Adlerian theory and system is a relational and constructive psychology and psychotherapy.

> For Adler, persons must be ultimately understood in social context; it is in relationships that humans have their meaning.... Psychological theories tend to be either individualistic or collectivistic—in the former community disappears; in the latter, the individual disappears. Adler's views, on the other hand, are a healthy balance of the individual rooted in relationships. (Jones & Butman, 1991, p. 237)

Because Adlerian theory/therapy clearly parallels many foundational ideas in both cognitive constructivist and social constructionist approaches, we believe the Adlerian model meets Neimeyer's (2000) criteria for designation as a relational constructivist approach.

The beauty of the Adlerian approach is its flexibility. Adlerians can be both theoretically integrative, albeit consistent, and technically eclectic. Different clients may require different therapeutic metaphors. One client may prefer a narrative-oriented approach, another a solution-focused orientation, and yet another a cognitive-behavioral or systemic one. Adlerian therapy allows the therapist to do whatever is in the best interest of his or her clients, rather than forcing clients—and their unique situations—into one therapeutic framework (Watts, 2000).

Adlerian and constructive therapies have much in common and much to offer each other. Given the contemporary integrationist zeitgeist, all of us—theorists, practitioners, and, more importantly, our clients—will benefit from continuing constructive dialogues.

REFERENCES

Adler, A. (1929). *Problems of neurosis* (P. Mairet, Ed.). London: Kegan Paul, Trench, Trubner.
Adler, A. (1992). *What life could mean to you* (C. Brett, Trans.). Oxford, UK: Oneworld Publications. (Original work published 1931)
Ainsworth, M. D. (1964). Patterns of attachment behavior shown by the infant in interactions with his mother. *Merrill Palmer Quarterly, 10,* 51–58.
Allen, T. W. (1971). A life style. *The Counseling Psychologist, 3,* 25–29.
Ansbacher, H. L. (1983). Individual Psychology. In R. J. Corsini & A. J. Marsella (Eds.), *Personality theories, research, & assessment* (pp. 69–123). Itasca, IL: Peacock.
Ansbacher, H. L., & Ansbacher, R. R. (Eds.). (1956). *The Individual Psychology of Alfred Adler: A systematic presentation in selections from his writings.* New York: Harper Torchbooks.

Ansbacher, H. L., & Ansbacher, R. R. (Eds.). (1978). *Cooperation between the sexes: Writings on women, love, and marriage.* New York: Norton.

Ansbacher, H. L., & Ansbacher, R. R. (Eds.). (1979). *Superiority and social interest: A collection of Alfred Adler's later writings* (3rd ed.). New York: Norton.

Arciniega, G. M., & Newlon, B. J. (1999). Counseling and psychotherapy: Multicultural considerations. In D. Capuzzi & D. F. Gross (Eds.), *Counseling & psychotherapy: Theories and interventions* (2nd ed., pp. 435–458). Upper Saddle River, NJ: Merrill/Prentice Hall.

Baruth, L., & Eckstein, D. (1981). *Life style: Theory, practice, and research* (2nd ed.). Dubuque, IA: Kendall/Hunt.

Bitter, J. R. (1997). Adlerian therapy: A foundation for integration. *Individual Psychology, 53,* 371–372.

Bowlby, J. (1982). *Attachment and loss: Vol. 1. Attachment* (2nd ed.). New York: Basic Books.

Carlson, J., & Dinkmeyer, D. (1999). Couple therapy. In R. E. Watts & J. Carlson (Eds.), *Interventions and strategies in counseling and psychotherapy* (pp. 87–99). Philadelphia: Accelerated Development/Taylor & Francis.

Carlson, J., & Slavik, S. (Eds.). (1997). *Techniques in Adlerian psychology.* Washington, DC: Accelerated Development.

Carlson, J., & Sperry, L. (1998). Adlerian psychotherapy as a constructivist psychotherapy. In M. F. Hoyt (Ed.), *The handbook of constructive therapies: Innovative approaches from leading practitioners* (pp. 68–82). San Francisco: Jossey-Bass.

Christensen, O. C. (Ed.). (1993). *Adlerian family counseling.* Minneapolis, MN: Educational Media.

Corey, G. (1996). *Theory and practice of counseling and psychotherapy* (5th ed.). Pacific Grove, CA: Brooks/Cole.

DeJong, P., & Berg, I. K. (1998). *Interviewing for solutions.* Pacific Grove, CA: Brooks/Cole.

de Shazer, S. (1991). *Putting differences to work.* New York: Norton.

Dinkmeyer, D. (1971). The "C" group: Integrating knowledge and experience to change behavior. *The Counseling Psychologist, 3,* 63–72.

Dinkmeyer, D. (1972). Use of the encouragement process in Adlerian counseling. *Personnel & Guidance Journal, 51,* 177–181.

Dinkmeyer, D., & Carlson, J. (1984). *Time for a better marriage.* Circle Pines, MN: American Guidance Service.

Dinkmeyer, D. C., Dinkmeyer, D. C., Jr., & Sperry, L. (1987). *Adlerian counseling and psychotherapy* (2nd ed.). Columbus, OH: Merrill.

Dinkmeyer, D., & Dreikurs, R. (1963). *Encouraging children to learn.* Englewood Cliffs, NJ: Prentice-Hall.

Dinkmeyer, D., & Losoncy, L. E. (1980). *The encouragement book.* Englewood Cliffs, NJ: Prentice-Hall.

Dinkmeyer, D., McKay, G. D., Dinkmeyer, D., Jr., Dinkmeyer, J. S., & McKay, J. L. (1987). *The effective parent.* Circle Pines, MN: American Guidance Service.

Dinkmeyer, D. C., & Muro, J. J. (1971). *Group counseling: Theory and practice.* Itasca, IL: Peacock.

Dinkmeyer, D., Jr., & Sperry, L. (2000). *Counseling and psychotherapy: An integrated, Individual Psychology approach* (3rd ed.). Upper Saddle River, NJ: Merrill/Prentice Hall.

Disque, J. G., & Bitter, J. R. (1998). Integrating narrative therapy with Adlerian lifestyle assessment: A case study. *Journal of Individual Psychology, 54,* 431–450.

Dreikurs, R. (1967). *Psychodynamics, psychotherapy, and counseling.* Chicago, IL: Alfred Adler Institute of Chicago.

Dreikurs, R. (1968). *Psychology in the classroom.* New York: Harper & Row.

Dreikurs, R. (1971). *Social equality: The challenge for today.* Chicago, IL: Adler School of Professional Psychology.

Dreikurs, R., & Soltz, V. (1964). *Children: The challenge.* New York: Hawthorn.

Eckstein, D., Baruth, L., & Mahrer, D. (1982). *Life style: What it is and how to do it* (2nd ed.). Dubuque, IA: Kendall/Hunt.

Ellenberger, H. F. (1970). *The discovery of the unconscious.* New York: Basic Books.

Forgus, R., & Shulman, B. H. (1979). *Personality: A cognitive view.* Englewood Cliffs, NJ: Prentice-Hall.

Gergen, K. J. (1994). *Realities and relationships: Soundings in social construction.* Cambridge, MA: Harvard University Press.

Gergen, K. J. (1999). *An invitation to social construction.* Thousand Oaks, CA: Sage.

Grizzle, A. F. (1992). Family therapy with the faithful: Christians as clients. In L. A. Burton (Ed.), *Religion and the family: When God helps* (pp. 139–162). New York: Haworth Pastoral Press.

Grunwald, B. (1971). Strategies for behavior change in schools. *The Counseling Psychologist, 3,* 55–57.

Grunwald, B. B., & McAbee, H. V. (1985). *Guiding the family.* Muncie, IN: Accelerated Development.

Guidano, V. F. (1991). *The self in process: Toward a post-rationalist cognitive therapy.* New York: Guilford.

Guidano, V. F. (1995a). A constructivist outline of human knowing processes. In M. J. Mahoney (Ed.), *Cognitive and constructive psychotherapies: Theory, research, and practice* (pp. 89–102). New York: Springer.

Guidano, V. F. (1995b). Constructivist psychotherapy: A theoretical framework. In R. A. Neimeyer & M. J. Mahoney (Eds.), *Constructivism in psychotherapy* (pp. 93–110). Washington, DC: American Psychological Association.

Guidano, V. F., & Liotti, G. (1983). *Cognitive process and emotional disorders.* New York: Guilford.

Guidano, V. F., & Liotti, G. (1985). A constructivistic foundation for cognitive therapy. In M. J. Mahoney & A. Freeman (Eds.), *Cognition and psychotherapy* (pp. 101–142). New York: Plenum.

Gushurst, R. S. (1971). The technique, utility, and validity of life style analysis. *The Counseling Psychologist, 3,* 30–39.

Hoffman, E. (1994). *The drive for self: Alfred Adler and the founding of individual psychology.* Reading, MA: Addison-Wesley.

Hoyt, M. F. (Ed.). (1994). *Constructive therapies.* New York: Guilford.

Hoyt, M. F. (Ed.). (1996). *Constructive therapies: Vol. 2.* New York: Guilford.

Hoyt, M. F. (Ed.). (1998). *The handbook of constructive therapies: Innovative approaches from leading practitioners*. San Francisco: Jossey-Bass.

Hubble, M. A., Duncan, B. L., & Miller, S. D. (Eds.). (1999). *The heart and soul of change: What works in therapy*. Washington, DC: American Psychological Association.

Jones, J. V., Jr. (1995). Constructivism and Individual Psychology: Common ground for dialogue. *Individual Psychology, 51*, 231–243.

Jones, S. L., & Butman, R. E. (1991). *Modern psychotherapies: A comprehensive Christian appraisal*. Downers Grove, IL: InterVarsity Press.

Kelly, G. (1955). *The psychology of personal constructs* (2 vols.). New York: Norton.

Kern, R. M., Hawes, E. C., & Christensen, O. C. (1989). *Couples therapy: An Adlerian perspective*. Minneapolis, MN: Educational Media.

Kottman, T. (1995). *Partners in play: An Adlerian approach to play therapy*. Alexandria, CA: American Counseling Association.

LaFountain, R. M. (1996). Social interest: A key to solutions. *Individual Psychology, 52*, 150–157.

LaFountain, R. M., & Garner, N. E. (1998). *A school with solutions: Implementing a solution-focused/Adlerian based comprehensive school counseling program*. Alexandria, VA: American School Counselor Association.

LaFountain, R. M., & Mustaine, B. L. (1998). Infusing Adlerian theory into an introductory marriage and family course. *The Family Journal, 6*, 189–199.

Littrell, J. M. (1998). *Brief counseling in action*. New York: Norton.

Lyddon, W. J. (1995). Forms and facets of constructivist psychology. In R. A. Neimeyer & M. J. Mahoney (Eds.), *Constructivism in psychotherapy* (pp. 69–92). Washington, DC: American Psychological Association.

Mahoney, M. J. (1988). Constructive metatheory: Basic features and historical foundations. *International Journal of Personal Construct Psychology, 1*, 1–35.

Mahoney, M. J. (1991). *Human change processes*. New York: Basic Books.

Mahoney, M. J. (1995a). Theoretical developments in cognitive and constructive psychotherapies. In M. J. Mahoney (Ed.), *Cognitive and constructive psychotherapies: Theory, research, and practice* (pp. 2–19). New York: Springer.

Mahoney, M. J. (1995b). Continuing evolution of the cognitive sciences and psychotherapies. In R. A. Neimeyer & M. J. Mahoney (Eds.), *Constructivism in psychotherapy* (pp. 39–68). Washington, DC: American Psychological Association.

Mahoney, M. J., Miller, H. M., & Arciero, G. (1995). Constructive metatheory and the nature of mental representation. In M. J. Mahoney (Ed.), *Cognitive and constructive psychotherapies: Theory, research, and practice* (pp. 103–120). New York: Springer.

Manaster, G. J., & Corsini, R. J. (1982). *Individual Psychology: Theory and practice*. Itasca, IL: Peacock.

Mansager, E. (Ed.). (2000). Holism, wellness, spirituality [Special Issue]. *Journal of Individual Psychology, 56*(3).

Maturana, H., & Varela, F. (1980). *Autopoiesis and cognition*. Boston: Reidel.

Master, S. B. (1991). Constructivism and the creative power of the self. *Individual Psychology, 47*, 447–455.

Mosak, H. H. (1971). Strategies for behavior change in schools: Consultation strategies. *The Counseling Psychologist, 3,* 58–62.
Mosak, H. H. (1979). Adlerian psychotherapy. In R. J. Corsini (Ed.), *Current psychotherapies* (2nd ed., pp. 44–94). Itasca, IL: Peacock.
Mosak, H. H. (1995). Adlerian psychotherapy. In R. J. Corsini & D. Wedding (Eds.), *Current psychotherapies* (5th ed., pp. 51–94). Itasca, IL: Peacock.
Mosak, H. H., & Maniacci, M. P. (1998). *Tactics in counseling and psychotherapy.* Itasca, IL: Peacock.
Mosak, H. H., & Maniacci, M. (1999). *A primer of Adlerian psychology: The analytic-behavioral-cognitive psychology of Alfred Adler.* Philadelphia: Accelerated Development/Taylor and Francis.
Mozdzierz, G. J. (1998). Culture, tradition, transition, and the future. *Journal of Individual Psychology, 54,* 275–277.
Neimeyer, G. J. (1995). The challenge of change. In R. A. Neimeyer & M. J. Mahoney (Eds.), *Constructivism in psychotherapy* (pp. 111–126). Washington, DC: American Psychological Association.
Neimeyer, R. A. (1995a). An invitation to constructivist psychotherapies. In R. A. Neimeyer & M. J. Mahoney (Eds.), *Constructivism in psychotherapy* (pp. 1–10). Washington, DC: American Psychological Association.
Neimeyer, R. A. (1995b). Constructivist psychotherapies: Features, foundations, and future directions. In R. A. Neimeyer & M. J. Mahoney (Eds.), *Constructivism in psychotherapy* (pp. 11–38). Washington, DC: American Psychological Association.
Neimeyer, R. A. (2000). Narrative disruptions in the construction of the self. In R. A. Neimeyer & J. D. Raskin (Eds.), *Constructions of disorder: Meaning-making frameworks for psychotherapy* (pp. 207–242). Washington, DC: American Psychological Association.
Neimeyer, R. A., & Mahoney, M. J. (1995). Glossary. In R. A. Neimeyer & M. J. Mahoney (Eds.), *Constructivism in psychotherapy* (pp. 401–409). Washington, DC: American Psychological Association.
Neimeyer, R. A., & Raskin, J. D. (Eds.). (2000). *Constructions of disorder: Meaning-making frameworks for psychotherapy.* Washington, DC: American Psychological Association.
Neuer, A. (1936). Courage and discouragement. *International Journal of Individual Psychology, 2*(2), 30–50.
O'Hanlon, W. H., & Weiner-Davis, M. (1989). *In search of solutions: A new direction in psychotherapy.* New York: Norton.
Parry, A., & Doan, R. E. (1994). *Story revisions: Narrative therapy in a postmodern world.* New York: Guilford.
Peluso, P. R., White, J. F., & Kern, R. M. (2002). *A comparison of attachment theory and Individual Psychology: A review of the literature.* [Manuscript submitted for publication].
Powers, R. L., & Griffith, J. (1987). *Understanding life-style: The psycho-clarity process.* Chicago: Americas Institute of Adlerian Studies.
Propst, L. R. (1996). Cognitive-behavioral therapy and the religious person. In E. P. Shafranske (Ed.), *Religion and the clinical practice of psychology* (pp. 391–408). Washington, DC: American Psychological Association.

Schneider, M. F., & Stone, M. (Eds.). (1998). Narrative therapy and Adlerian psychology [Special issue]. *Journal of Individual Psychology, 54*(4).

Scott, C. N., Kelly, F. D., & Tolbert, B. L. (1995). Realism, constructivism, and the Individual Psychology of Alfred Adler. *Individual Psychology, 51*, 4–20.

Sherman, R. (1999). Family therapy: The art of integration. In R. E. Watts & J. Carlson (Eds.), *Interventions and strategies in counseling and psychotherapy* (pp. 101–134). Philadelphia: Accelerated Development/Taylor & Francis.

Sherman, R., & Dinkmeyer, D. (1987). *Systems of family therapy: An Adlerian integration.* New York: Brunner/Mazel.

Shulman, B. H. (1973). *Contributions to Individual Psychology.* Chicago: The Alfred Adler Institute.

Shulman, B. H. (1985). Cognitive therapy and the Individual Psychology of Alfred Adler. In M. J. Mahoney & A. Freeman (Eds.), *Cognition and psychotherapy* (pp. 243–258). New York: Plenum.

Shulman, B. H., & Mosak, H. H. (1988). *Handbook for the life style.* Muncie, IN: Accelerated Development.

Stepansky, P. E. (1983). *In Freud's shadow: Adler in context.* London: The Analytic Press.

Sweeney, T. J. (1998). *Adlerian counseling: A practitioner's approach* (4th ed.). Muncie, IN: Accelerated Development.

Walter, J. L., & Peller, J. E. (1992). *Becoming solution-focused in brief therapy.* New York: Brunner/Mazel.

Watts, R. E. (1998). The remarkable similarity between Rogers's core conditions and Adler's social interest. *Journal of Individual Psychology, 54*, 4–9.

Watts, R. E. (1999). The vision of Adler: An introduction. In R. E. Watts & J. Carlson (Eds.), *Interventions and strategies in counseling and psychotherapy* (pp. 1–13). Philadelphia: Accelerated Development/Taylor & Francis.

Watts, R. E. (2000). Entering the new millennium: Is Individual Psychology/Adlerian therapy still relevant? *Journal of Individual Psychology, 56*, 21–30.

Watts, R. E., & Carlson, J. (Eds.). (1999). *Interventions and strategies in counseling and psychotherapy.* Philadelphia: Accelerated Development/Taylor & Francis.

Watts, R. E., & Critelli, J. W. (1997). Roots of contemporary cognitive theories in the Individual Psychology of Alfred Adler. *Journal of Cognitive Psychotherapy, 11*, 147–156.

Watts, R. E., & Pietrzak, D. (2000). Adlerian "encouragement" and the therapeutic process of solution-focused brief therapy. *Journal of Counseling and Development, 78*, 442–447.

White, M., & Epston, D. (1990). *Narrative means to therapeutic ends.* New York: Norton.

3

Adlerian and Constructivist Psychotherapies: A Constructivist Perspective

John V. Jones, Jr. and William J. Lyddon

These are exciting times, as psychotherapy theorists and practitioners seek to draw from different perspectives to solidify their philosophical assumptions about human nature and to become more efficient agents of change in their day-to-day practices. In this chapter, we hope to contribute to a continuing dialogue between Adlerians and constructivists (Jones, 1995; Master, 1991; Scott, Kelly, & Brandon, 1995). Both camps have much in common, but we believe each perspective also has unique features to offer the other.

ADLERIAN AND CONSTRUCTIVIST SIMILARITIES

The similarities between Adlerian and constructivist approaches to psychotherapy can be discussed along philosophical, theoretical, and practical considerations. The commonalities provide rich and fertile common ground for an integrative dialogue.

Philosophical Similarities

Phenomenology

Both Adlerians and constructivists tend to adhere to a phenomenological framework. Both camps point to Kant (1781/1966) and Vaihinger

(1911/1924) as formative philosophical influences. For constructivists, Kant provides the philosophical basis for their view of the human mind as an active and proactive construer of reality (Mahoney, 1988a, 1988b, 1991; Neimeyer, 1995). This constructive view of the mind coincides with the phenomenological position of intentionality developed by Brentano (1874/1973) and Husserl (1931/1962). The early constructivist, George Kelly (1955), also looked to Vaihinger's philosophy of "as if," with its emphasis on a purposive mind, as a source for his notion of an anticipatory mind as theorized in personal construct psychology. Constructivists also suggest that, even though a person constructs a mental representation of reality, there is not a one-to-one correspondence between the mental representation and reality. However, constructivists point out that, for the person to adapt and survive, mental representations must approximate reality. Hence, constructivists tend to embrace Popper's (1983) critical realism and Campbell's (1987) evolutionary epistemology. Additionally, the person's continuous interaction with the world enables the development of the self (Mahoney, 1991; Mahoney & Lyddon, 1988). So, constructivists also tend to view the individual in developmental terms as a continuous self-in-process.

Adler, likewise, looked to Vaihinger's philosophy of "as if" as a source for his phenomenological and teleological view of human nature (Ansbacher & Ansbacher, 1956). The fictional goals that a person constructs are interpretations of the world as experienced by that individual. Although these fictions cannot be assessed as to whether they correspond to reality, they enable a person to adapt and move purposely toward selected goals. Because these fictional goals are never realized, Adlerians tend to view the individual not as static, but as one who is in continuous movement, always becoming (Ansbacher & Ansbacher, 1956).

Holism

The holistic approach of both Adlerians and constructivists provides fertile soil for an integrative dialogue, particularly in the area of what both camps consider to be false dichotomies. Mahoney (1991), for example, in his discussion of the history of ideas, suggests that such distinctions as ontology–epistemology, structure–function, mind–body, and subjective–objective involve false dichotomies that misrepresent the holistic, organic functioning of the human being. Constructivists view the person as an "anticipatory 'embodied theory' " (Mahoney, 1991, p.

100). They reject a reductionistic, parts-function view of the individual. Consequently, constructivists embrace the work of Popper and Eccles (1977) on mind–body interaction, and the work of Weimer (1977), whose motor theory of the mind challenges traditional views of the mind based on the separation of sensory and motor functions (Mahoney, 1991; Mahoney & Lyddon, 1988).

Likewise, Adlerians view polarities such as mind–body and conscious–unconscious as false dichotomies (Mosak, 1989). For Adlerians, holism represents a rejection of reductionism and the dissection of the human into parts. Adler's notion of *psychology of use* (functionalism) derives from his holistic approach. According to Adler, all so-called parts or functions of the individual are subordinated to the individual's goals or lifestyle (Ansbacher & Ansbacher, 1956). All components that presumably comprise the personality are believed to function holistically.

Existentialism and Meaning

Both Adlerians and constructivists emphasize the fundamental role of meaning-making activity in human experience. Constructivists find common ground with the logotherapist Frankl (1984) and his notion that personal meaning forms the key to an individual's psychological well-being (Mahoney, 1991). All of the experiences that go into a person's construction of reality involve the individual's interpretation and organization of those experiences into a meaningful whole. Personal constructs are key to understanding the individual, because they are imbued with personal meaning (Mahoney, 1991).

Adlerians view individuals as both free and responsible in selecting the goals by which they move through life. The selection of goals that make up the lifestyle involves the individual's values and personal meaning (Ansbacher & Ansbacher, 1956; Mosak, 1989). Adlerians believe that people create their meaning in a world where meaning may not be intrinsic; consequently, people's actions can be understood in terms of the meaning they create. A person's style of life is derived from the meaning he or she creates (Mosak, 1989).

Theoretical Similarities

Both Adlerians and constructivists share theoretical positions that can be delineated as cognitive and ecological. Additionally, both Adlerians and constructivists emphasize the importance of family of origin and early childhood experiences in the makeup of an individual's style of life or personal constructs. Finally, both approaches share a common view of the phenomenon commonly termed *resistance*.

Cognitive Approach

Adlerian psychology, as a cognitive approach, has been documented by several theorists (Forgus & Shulman, 1979; Mosak, 1989; Shulman, 1985). Mosak (1989) equated the Adlerian concept of *lifestyle* with the individual's cognitive organization, which comprises the individual's basic convictions. Based on what Adler called a *schema* of apperception, people interpret their subjective experiences and derive conclusions and basic convictions about life (Ansbacher & Ansbacher, 1956). According to Adlerians, lifestyle changes occur only when changes in basic convictions occur. Mosak (1989) also pointed out that one's cognitive organization or style of life is usually out of awareness. Compared to Freud's view of the unconscious, Adlerians view the unconscious or nonconscious as that which one does not completely understand. Succinctly stated, Adlerian psychotherapy involves helping clients gain insight into their cognitive organization, basic convictions, or style of life.

Constructivists describe cognitive organization in terms of core (or superordinate) and peripheral (or subordinate) constructs (Guidano & Liotti, 1983; Kelly, 1955; Mahoney, 1991; Safran & Segal, 1990; Safran, Vallis, Segal, & Shaw, 1986). Core constructs make up what constructivists designate as *tacit knowledge*, which is similar to the Adlerian notion of the nonconscious. Tacit knowledge is an out-of-awareness framework that constrains a person's explicit knowledge (peripheral constructs) (Guidano & Liotti, 1983; Mahoney, 1991; Polanyi, 1967). For constructivists, core or second-order change, similar to the Adlerian idea of lifestyle change, involves individuals becoming aware of fundamental assumptions about the self, world, and relationships, so that the choice to both challenge and change these assumptions becomes available (Lyddon, 1990; Mahoney, 1991).

Historically, constructivism has been contrasted with traditional cognitive therapies, such as Ellis's (1994) rational-emotive behavior and Beck's (1976) cognitive therapy (Mahoney, 1991). Mahoney (1991), Lyddon (1988, 1990), and Neimeyer (1995) distinguish a cognitive-constructive approach from a traditional, rationalist, information-processing approach. One prominent difference cited between the two approaches involves the constructivist's use of emotion, early childhood experiences, and less of an emphasis on cognitive supremacy. More recently, however, cognitive approaches have embraced constructivist notions of development and emotion (e.g., Layden, Newman, Freeman, & Morse, 1993).

Ecological Approach

Both Adlerians and constructivists believe that human existence takes place in an interpersonal and a social context. Adlerians strongly emphasize the interpersonal nature of their approach, employing concepts such as social embeddedness, social feeling, and social interest (Ansbacher & Ansbacher, 1956, 1979; Mosak, 1989). Indeed, for Adlerians, social interest becomes the standard by which one's style of life is gauged, as to whether it is adaptive or maladaptive (Ansbacher & Ansbacher, 1956, 1979; Manaster & Corsini, 1982). Hence, Adlerians contend that people cannot be understood apart from their social context.

Two constructivists, Safran (1984a, 1984b, 1990a, 1990b) and Segal (Safran & Segal, 1990), have integrated the interpersonal psychiatry of Sullivan (1953) within a cognitive approach. In place of an information-processing view of cognition, Safran and Segal (1990) employed Bateson's (1972) ecological view of people as proactive information seekers and interactors with their environment. Safran and Segal's cognitive-interpersonal approach recognizes that the most important interactions within one's environment involve other people. Consequently, the beliefs that one construes about oneself are derived from interpersonal interactions.

Family of Origin

Both Adlerians and constructivists believe that family of origin and early childhood experiences contribute to an understanding a person's style of life or system of constructs. Indeed, Adler (Ansbacher & Ansbacher, 1956; Mosak, 1989) suggested that one's style of life was, for the most part, set by the age of 6 years, and remained fairly constant throughout one's life. Hence, Adlerians employ the use of early recollections, consider birth-order dynamics, and explore family-of-origin experiences, in order to help clients gain insight into their basic convictions or style of life (Ansbacher & Ansbacher, 1956, 1979; Mosak, 1989). Adlerians frequently use a lifestyle analysis as a tool for helping clients become aware of their basic convictions and private logic (Sweeney, 1989).

Constructivists also believe that early experiences contribute to the construction of beliefs about self, world, and relationships (Guidano & Liotti, 1983; Liotti, 1984, 1987; Mahoney, 1991; Safran et al., 1986). For example, constructivists have used attachment theory (Bowlby, 1969, 1973, 1979, 1980, 1988; Holmes, 1993) in order to understand the patterns by which people approach interpersonal relationships. An assessment of clients' attachment patterns or interpersonal styles often provides therapists with important information bearing on the client's core constructs, which may no longer be viable in light of new developmental challenges (Lyddon & Alford, 1993). Guidano and Liotti (1983), for example, suggest that certain disorders tend to be correlated with particular patterns of insecure attachment.

Resistance

Adlerians and constructivists also concur on how to understand and approach the phenomenon of resistance in therapy. Many Adlerians use the term *safeguarding*, instead of resistance, because they view resistant clients as employing coping mechanisms to protect themselves against feelings of inferiority (Mosak, 1989). These coping mechanisms safeguard an individual's self-worth or self-esteem.

Similarly, constructivists view a client's resistance to therapy as a self-protective measure. From a constructivist perspective, a resistant client is protecting core beliefs that have been useful and adaptive to a point. Because these core beliefs are related to self or identity, it is natural for clients to protect the integrity of the self-system when it is threatened by new information and possibilities (Guidano & Liotti, 1983; Mahoney, 1991). Consequently, for both Adlerians and constructivists, resistance signals a process that therapists should work with, not against (Mahoney, 1991).

Practical Considerations

Because Adlerians and constructivists share common philosophical and theoretical positions, both have similar views of how to approach the day-to-day task of doing therapy. In particular, Adlerians and constructivists tend to have similar conceptions of the therapeutic relationship, assessment, and psychotherapeutic techniques.

Therapeutic Relationship

Adlerians believe in a therapeutic relationship that is egalitarian and collaborative in nature, in order to encourage and empower clients to reach their own conclusions and solve their own problems. According to Adlerians, without a trusting and safe therapeutic relationship, counseling will not proceed in a fruitful manner (Mosak, 1989; Sweeney, 1989).

Because many constructivists integrate Bowlby's (1988) concept of a *secure base* into their theoretical framework, they seek to provide a safe therapeutic environment that allows clients to explore, take chances, and risk the paths of change. Guidano and Liotti (1983), for example, describe the therapeutic relationship as secure and collaborative. For constructivists, the absence of a secure base undermines the efforts of therapy (Guidano & Liotti, 1983; Mahoney, 1991).

Assessment

Because both Adlerians and constructivists take a process view of the individual, they do not understand assessment as a static event that occurs before work with the client begins. Assessment is always in process. Adlerians perform lifestyle analyses (Mosak, 1989; Sweeney, 1989); constructivists seek to uncover patterns of attachment used in the assessment of core processes (Guidano & Liotti, 1983). Both Adlerians (Sweeney, 1989) and constructivists (Neimeyer, 1993) employ a variety of assessment techniques that tend to be more qualitative and idiographic than quantitative and nomothetic. Both Adlerians and constructivists utilize the *Diagnostic and statistical manual of mental disorders*, 4th ed., Text Revised (2000) but recognize that diagnoses do not mean that individuals fall into a diagnostic category that leads to formulaic therapy.

Techniques

Both Adlerians and constructivists use a variety of cognitive, behavioral, and experiential techniques that stem specifically from their respective theoretical bases. The common thread that binds both camps is their use of techniques to provide situations for new learning, that is, opportunities to experience new information that is discrepant with existing cognitive structures or lifestyle. For Adlerians, the aim of psychotherapy is to provide insight into basic convictions that form the person's lifestyle. Acting as if, spitting in the client's soup, and the push-button technique are examples of Adlerian techniques that provide clients with new information into how their lifestyle works in day-to-day life (Mosak, 1989; Sweeney, 1989). Only when such awareness or insight has been developed can clients decide how to assimilate or accommodate this new information, thereby modifying or possibly revolutionizing their style of life. For constructivists, the aim of psychotherapy is to produce new learning via novel situations that provide contrasts to existing cognitive structures (Lyddon, 1993). Repertory grids and fixed role therapy (Kelly, 1955), self-narratives (Neimeyer, 1995), and experiential techniques, such as streaming and the mirror dialogue (Mahoney, 1991), provide clients opportunities to experiment with novel situations that may foster new learning.

Although the philosophical, theoretical, and practical similarities provide rich opportunities for an integrative dialogue between Adlerians and constructivists, each camp also possesses unique features and concepts. We now turn to a discussion of these features and what we believe each camp can offer the other in terms of understanding human experiences and human beings.

CONSTRUCTIVIST GLEANINGS FROM ADLERIAN PSYCHOLOGY

Although there are probably many Adlerian avenues that might provide some fruitful traveling for constructivists, both theoretically and practically, we focus here on three areas: teleology and the striving for significance, social interest, and family-of-origin and lifestyle analysis.

Teleology and the Striving for Significance

Adlerians conceptualize human behavior in terms of compensatory striving for superiority that originates in feelings of inferiority relative to early childhood and family-of-origin experiences. This ceaseless striving characterizes the dynamic process that, for Adlerians, is human existence. Other terms used to describe this process include *striving for perfection* or *striving for significance* (Ansbacher & Ansbacher, 1956).

Adler believed the compensatory striving to be universal, based on individual subjective goals, and to involve either a healthy or unhealthy dynamic. Although Adler derived his concept of superiority from

Nietzsche's (1911/1967) superman with the "will to power," he spoke of superiority in a more benevolent sense. For Adler, striving for superiority in the healthy sense involves developing personal skills to master life tasks. Malevolent superiority involves the attempt to control others (Ansbacher & Ansbacher, 1956).

Because both Adlerians and constructivists claim common ground relative to phenomenology and the proactive nature of the human being, constructivists may find the Adlerian construct of purposive behavior useful. Both camps concur that behavior is directional and anticipatory. Constructivists talk, however, more in terms of adaptation when speaking of directional behavior. Indeed, Mahoney (1991) used the term *teleonomic*, instead of teleological, to describe the adaptive anticipatory nature of human action. By incorporating Adler's concept of social adaptive striving into their theoretical framework, constructivists may find that they do not have to give up their teleonomic view of human action. More importantly, Adlerians and constructivists can communicate on the integration of teleonomy and teleology. Lyddon and McLaughlin (1992), for example, theorized that, among several forms of constructivism, "final" constructivism presupposes that knowledge is fundamentally teleological, by its anticipatory nature. In this regard, Adler's concept of compensatory striving appears to mesh well with Kelly's (1955) concept of anticipatory behavior and his person-as-scientist metaphor. Moreover, Adler's concept of striving for significance underscores what is fundamental to both camps: the meaning-making activity of the individual. Because Adlerians view striving for significance is predicated on what is purposeful and meaningful to the individual, constructivists may be able to utilize this conceptual tool to augment their notion of how novel experiences may challenge a client's personal meaning.

Social Interest

Adler held that people are social beings, and that they are born to be social (Ansbacher & Ansbacher, 1979). Social interest, for Adlerians, is the gauge by which an individual's lifestyle is assessed as either useful or useless. Those who pursue their life goals in a cooperative spirit with others evidence social interest. Social interest is not a mere component of Adlerian theory. It is the dynamic by which Adlerian theory is understood as an organismic, holistic theory. Although social embeddedness underlies the importance of understanding the person in context, social interest is considered by Adlerians to be innate, but an innate substratum that must be developed in the midst of life. Social interest gives positive direction to the upward striving of the human being and describes why connectedness is important to well-being (Ansbacher & Ansbacher, 1979; Manaster & Corsini, 1982; Mosak, 1989; Sweeney, 1989).

Constructivists may want to look to Adlerian theory in terms of the social understanding of the individual. Although Kelly (1955) employed the sociality corollary in his personal construct theory, his theory was viewed as emphasizing the individual. Other constructivists (Guidano & Liotti, 1983; Mahoney, 1991), however, have integrated Bandura's (1977, 1986) social learning theory into their theoretical framework. Safran and Segal (1990), drawing on Sullivan (1953), emphasized the importance of the interpersonal context in understanding the individual. Some constructivist-oriented theorists have offered challenges to traditional individualist epistemologies, by recognizing the ways in which knowledge is socially constituted (Lyddon, 1991). Indeed, Gergen (1994), as a social constructionist, claims that all knowledge is social, and that the individual can be understood only in terms of the social. In addition to social constructionism, narrative psychology theorists with constructivist leanings (Efran, 1994; Goncalves, 1994a, 1994b; Mair, 1988, 1989, 1990; Neimeyer, 1994; Russel, 1991; Sarbin, 1986; van den Broek & Thurlow, 1991; Vogel, 1994; White & Epston, 1990) also challenge the decontextualized understandings of personal narratives. Indeed, Lyddon and McLaughlin (1992), in their discussion of four forms of constructivism, conceptualize both social constructionism and narrative psychology as contextual forms of constructivism that emphasize society's collective construction of reality. The Adlerian construct of social interest may prove to be a useful conceptual tool for constructivists who now emphasize socially constituted knowledge, as well as individually constructed knowledge. The positive spirit of cooperation with which Adler viewed social interest may also prove integrative with the constructivist concern for hope and active engagement, through what Mahoney (1985) terms *participatory vitalism*. Mahoney views hope as a vital factor in all life processes at both the individual and social levels. Because Adlerian theory is premised on social evolution, integrating the concept of social interest with Campbell's (1987) evolutionary epistemology may also prove fruitful.

Lifestyle Analysis

Adlerians perform a lifestyle analysis in order to understand the individual in the context of a family constellation (Ansbacher & Ansbacher, 1956, 1979; Dinkmeyer, Dinkmeyer, & Sperry, 1987; Manaster & Corsini, 1982; Sweeney, 1989). Lifestyle analyses provide information about parent–child relations, sibling relations, family environment, birth-order considerations, and early recollections. The lifestyle analysis is not intended to establish past, historical facts, but aims, instead, at establishing the client's selected memories and present interpretations of significant interactions and how those interpretations operate in the client's present world. Some constructivists focus on attachment patterns to assess present mental representations of interpersonal relationships (Guidano & Liotti, 1983; Lyddon & Alford, 1993), but lifestyle analyses and family constellations are additional sources of developmental and social information that may aid constructivists in assessing various dimensions of their clients' interpersonal realities.

USEFUL CONSTRUCTS FOR ADLERIANS

Neimeyer (1995) delineated several specific constructivist therapies that fall under the umbrella of the metatheory of constructivism. Because of the similarities discussed in the first section of this chapter, Adlerians can peruse the theoretical concepts and work of constructivists to find many useful tools for continued conceptualization and the progressive work of therapy. The ideas that strongly bind both camps are a belief in the progress of knowledge and the complementary notion that the work of understanding human nature is never completely done. Although the ideas presented here, which Adlerians may find useful, are not exhaustive, Adlerians may want to consider the constructivist emphases on structuralism, evolutionary epistemology and motor theory of the mind, attachment theory, and triadic reciprocality.

Structuralism

Adler emphasized the functional aspect of his theory, which he termed a "psychology of use" (Ansbacher & Ansbacher, 1956; Mosak, 1989). Because he rejected psychoanalytic reductionism and the partitioning of the personality into parts, Adler opposed Freud's structural conceptions.

But constructivists emphasize, like Adlerians, going beyond false dichotomies found in theoretical debates. Structuralism–functionalism, according to constructivists, is yet another questionable dichotomy in the debates about human nature (Mahoney, 1991). Hence, constructivists believe that structure and function are inseparable. Historically, models of the mind have been analogous to the technology within the zeitgeist in which the models were erected. Energy models, in Freud's time, included Newtonian mechanistic physics; information-processing models of the computer age offered input–output models that meshed with sensory metatheories of the mind. Presently, models of the mind are fashioned after research in cognitive science and neurophysiology (Mahoney, 1991; Mahoney & Lyddon, 1988). Coinciding with the spirit of holism, constructivists have embraced a motor theory of the mind (Weimer, 1977), which emphasizes the holistic, ecological, and enactive nature of the mind. Constructivist models are heterarchical in their emphasis on coalitional control structures and hierarchical in their delineation of core and peripheral constructs (Guidano & Liotti, 1983; Kelly, 1955; Mahoney, 1991; Safran & Segal, 1990; Safran et al., 1986; Vallis, 1991).

In addition to a holistic conception of the mind, there are other inroads for an integrative dialogue between constructivists and Adlerians in relation to structuralism. Core constructs have been viewed by some constructivists as analogous to the Adlerian concept of lifestyle (Mahoney, 1984, 1988a). In addition, constructivists fall within a more European view of structuralism, as delineated by Mahoney (1991). The American approach to structuralism has involved the search for a rigid architecture of the mind; the European view of structuralism posits a more dynamic and evolutionary approach to structure. This latter approach is a better fit for a view of the self-in-process and evolutionary epistemology (Campbell, 1987; Popper, 1987) embraced by constructivists. Evolutionary epistemology emphasizes the anticipatory activity of self-organization of the individual (Mahoney & Lyddon, 1988). Hence, another issue that may facilitate an integrative dialogue between Adlerians and constructivists with respect to structure and function, may involve the Adlerian concept of the creative powers of the self (Master, 1991) and the constructivist notion of the evolutionary self-in-process (Guidano, 1987, 1991).

Attachment Theory

Constructivists can benefit from the Adlerian practice of the lifestyle analysis, but they can also offer Adlerians some theoretical grist for the mill, in terms of attachment theory (Bowlby, 1969, 1973, 1979, 1980, 1988). Attachment theory is based on the notion that one of the biological contributions to the understanding of the human being is the need for love, in terms of touch, warmth, and security. A person's degree of attachment security contributes to that individual's phenomenological view of the world, particularly in the areas of interpersonal relationships. According to attachment theorists, one aim of purposive behavior is the seeking of interpersonal relationships to fulfill the type of attachment that may have been lacking in the family of origin. Hence, attachment theory can contribute to and be used to support Adlerian explanations of how an individual's style of life develops.

Guidano and Liotti (1983) have discussed correlations between types of insecure attachment between parents and children and particular pathologies in adolescents and adulthood. Safran and Segal (1990) have integrated attachment theory and Sullivan's (1953) interpersonal psychiatry into their cognitive-constructivist approach. Mahoney (1991) discussed attachment as it relates to the development of a person's core and tacit processes. Lyddon and his colleagues have studied the relations between client attachment and disordered eating (Friedberg & Lyddon, 1996), child sexual abuse (Schreiber & Lyddon, 1998), client coping resources (Buelow, Lyddon, & Johnson, 2002), personality disorders (Lyddon & Sherry, 2001), the working alliance (Satterfield & Lyddon, 1998), and therapist first- and second-order change assessments (Lyddon & Satterfield, 1994). Adlerians may want to explore the implications of attachment theory for clinical practice, especially when clients' early recollections involve themes of parental dominance, overprotection, neglect, or mixed messages of protection and neglect.

Social Learning Theory and Triadic Reciprocality

Because Individual Psychology is an insight-oriented theory, and because Adlerians focus on basic beliefs or convictions, the theory has integrated well with cognitive approaches (Forgus & Shulman, 1979; Shulman, 1985). Social learning theory (Bandura, 1977, 1986) provides another path for integrative dialogue between Adlerians and constructivists. Lyddon and McLaughlin (1992) pointed out that social learning theory is cognitive (rule-governed) and constructivist (interpretive). Additionally, social learning theory is contextual, in that it focuses on the individual in a social context.

An important concept in social learning theory involves the notion of the reciprocal interaction among cognition, behavior, and emotion. For constructivists, triadic reciprocality means that learning involves more than what occurs in the head. Emotion is a powerful form of knowing, particularly when structural or core change is involved. The concept of reciprocal interaction has also led constructivists to view emotion as something other than a problem to be solved in therapy. Instead, intense emotion often is a prerequisite to significant change, that is, something to be expected as one's systemic structure breaks down in the forming of another. Hence, instead of something to be cured, intense emotion can signal a path toward deep, tacit change (Mahoney, 1991). Because Adlerians, like constructivists, focus on holistic, organic, and individual processes, triadic reciprocality and this adaptive view of emotion represent additional features of constructivism that may enrich and resonate with contemporary Adlerians.

CONCLUSION: THEORETICAL INTEGRATION

In a dialogue between Adlerians and constructivists, we believe that three notions shared by both approaches may provide some paths for integration: teleology and meaning, contextualism, and holism. Adler's teleological concept of striving for significance augments constructivist concerns of knowledge as anticipatory and adaptive. Moreover, a telic view of human knowing presupposes that the individual is purposeful, creative, and a free agent. Such a perspective emphasizes an individual's meaning-making activity. Add to this concept the perspective that human knowing is socially constituted, then meaning-making systems, such as culture, history of ideas, religion, and art, take on supreme importance. Adler's perspective on the person as a social being meshes with the constructivist concern regarding traditional decontextualized understanding of the person. Furthermore, the Adlerian use of the lifestyle analysis, coupled with the constructivist emphasis on attachment behavior, suggests that each approach holds something that it can offer the other, to augment a contextual understanding of the individual.

Because both theories reflect a holistic approach, pathways of integration should lie along each theory's approach to the mind–body problem. Both approaches emphasize a position of interaction, but, while Adlerian theorists have emphasized a functional approach, constructivists have sought to go beyond the structural–functional dichotomy, offering a dynamic and an evolutionary embodiment theory. The constructivists bring to the dialogue the findings of research in cognitive science and neurophysiology. Likewise, constructivists have integrated Popper (1987) and Campbell's (1987) evolutionary epistemology, and Weimer's (1977) motor metatheory of the mind into their theoretical framework, all of which emphasize the evolutionary, ecological, and enactive nature of the human mind and the attempt to integrate structure and function. The constructivist perspective of the self-in-process and the Adlerian concept of the creative powers of the self form a common ground for both camps to consider the issues of functionalism and structuralism. An additional concern in relation to holism is the constructivist perspective of emotion, based on Bandura's (1977, 1986) concept of triadic reciprocality. This systemic perspective views emotion as an adaptive mechanism inherent in the change process, particularly revolutionary change. Because both constructivists and Adlerians hold a similar view of the role of novel experiences and the change process (e.g., confirming or not confirming core structures or lifestyle), the constructivist notion of the disequilibrating function of such novel experiences may augment Adlerians' view of the change process, to include a more adaptive and developmental role for emotional "dis-ease" and disorder.

As theorists and practitioners continue to explore various modes of psychotherapy integration, we hope this chapter may both contribute to greater dialogue between Adlerian and constructivists and pique the interest of others to enter the dialogue. Adlerians and constructivists share many commonalities in their perspectives and approaches, yet both possess unique features. We believe that each can enrich the other, and, in so doing, contribute to a better understanding of human knowing and human change processes.

REFERENCES

Ansbacher, H. L., & Ansbacher, R. R. (Eds.). (1956). *The Individual Psychology of Alfred Adler: A systematic presentation in selections from his writings*. New York: Basic Books.

Ansbacher, H. L., & Ansbacher, R. R. (Eds.). (1979). *Superiority and social interest: A collection of Alfred Adler's later writings*. New York: Norton.

Bandura, A. (1977). *Social learning theory*. Englewood Cliffs, NJ: Prentice Hall.

Bandura, A. (1986). *Social foundations of thought and action: A social cognitive theory*. Englewood Cliffs, NJ: Prentice Hall.

Bateson, G. (1972). *Steps towards an ecology of the mind*. San Francisco: Chandler.

Beck, A. T. (1976). *Cognitive therapy and the emotional disorders.* New York: New American Library.
Bowlby, J. (1969). *Attachment and loss: Vol. I. Attachment.* New York: Basic Books.
Bowlby, J. (1973). *Attachment and loss: Vol. II. Separation.* New York: Basic Books.
Bowlby, J. (1979). *The making and breaking of affectional bonds.* New York: Routledge.
Bowlby, J. (1980). *Attachment and loss: Vol. III. Loss.* New York: Basic Books.
Bowlby, J. (1988). *A secure base: Parent–child attachment and healthy human development.* New York: Basic Books.
Brentano, F. (1973). *Psychology from an empirical standpoint* (A. C. Rancurello, Trans.). New York: Humanities Press. (Original work published 1874)
Buelow, S. A., Lyddon, W. J., & Johnson, J. T. (2002). Client attachment and coping resources. *Counseling Psychology Quarterly, 15,* 145–152.
Campbell, D. T. (1987). Evolutionary epistemology. In G. Radnitzky & W. W. Bartley III (Eds.), *Evolutionary epistemology, rationality, and the sociology of knowledge* (pp. 47–89). La Salle, IL: Open Court.
Dinkmeyer, D. C., Dinkmeyer, D. C., Jr., & Sperry, L. (1987). *Adlerian counseling and psychotherapy.* New York: Macmillan.
Efran, J. S. (1994). Mystery, abstraction, and narrative psychotherapy. *Journal of Constructivist Psychology, 7*(4), 219–228.
Ellis, A. (1994). *Reason and emotion in psychotherapy.* New York: Birch Lane Press.
Forgus, R., & Shulman, B. H. (1979). *Personality: A cognitive view.* Englewood Cliffs, NJ: Prentice Hall.
Frankl, V. (1984). *Man's search for meaning.* New York: Simon & Schuster.
Friedberg, N. L., & Lyddon, W. J. (1996). Self-other working models and eating disorders. *Journal of Cognitive Psychotherapy: An International Quarterly, 10,* 193–203.
Gergen, K. J. (1994). *Realities and relationships: Soundings in social construction.* Cambridge, MA: Harvard University Press.
Goncalves, O. F. (1994a). Cognitive narrative psychotherapy: The hermeneutic construction of alternative meanings. *Journal of Cognitive Psychotherapy, 8*(2), 105–125.
Goncalves, O. F. (1994b). From epistemological truth to existential meaning in cognitive narrative psychotherapy. *Journal of Constructivist Psychology, 7*(2), 107–118.
Guidano, V. F. (1987). *Complexity of the self.* New York: Guilford.
Guidano, V. F. (1991). *The self in process.* New York: Guilford.
Guidano, V. F., & Liotti, G. (1983). *Cognitive processes and emotional disorders.* New York: Guilford.
Holmes, J. (1993). *Makers of modern psychotherapy: John Bowlby and attachment theory.* New York: Routledge.
Husserl, E. (1962). *Ideas: General introduction to pure phenomenology* (W. R. B. Gibson, Trans.). New York: Collier. (Original work published 1931)
Jones, J. V. (1995). Individual Psychology and constructivism: Common ground for dialogue. *Individual Psychology, 5,* 231–243.
Kant, I. (1966). *Critique of pure reason* (F. M. Muller, Trans.). Garden City, NY: Doubleday. (Original work published 1781)

Kelly, G. (1955). *A theory of personality: The psychology of personal constructs.* New York: Norton.

Layden, M. A., Newman, C. F., Freeman, A., & Morse, S. B. (1993). *Cognitive therapy of borderline personality disorder.* Boston: Allyn & Bacon.

Liotti, G. (1984). Cognitive therapy, attachment theory, and psychiatric nosology. A clinical and theoretical inquiry into their interdependence. In M. Reda & M. J. Mahoney (Eds.), *Cognitive psychotherapies: Recent developments in theory, research, and practice* (pp. 211–231). Cambridge, MA: Ballinger.

Liotti, G. (1987). Structural cognitive therapy. In W. Dryden & W. Golden (Eds.), *Cognitive behavioral approaches to psychotherapy* (pp. 92–128). New York: Hemisphere.

Lyddon, W. J. (1988). Information-processing and constructivist models of cognitive therapy: A philosophical divergence. *The Journal of Mind and Behavior, 9*(2), 137–165.

Lyddon, W. J. (1990). First- and second-order change: Implications for rationalist and constructivist psychotherapies. *Journal of Counseling and Development, 69,* 122–127.

Lyddon, W. J. (1991). Socially constituted knowledge: Philosophical, psychological, and feminist contributions. *The Journal of Mind and Behavior, 12*(1), 263–279.

Lyddon, W. J. (1993). Contrast, contradiction, and change in psychotherapy. *Psychotherapy, 30,* 383–390.

Lyddon, W. J., & Alford, D. J. (1993). Constructivist assessment: A developmental-epistemic perspective. In G. J. Neimeyer (Ed.), *Casebook of constructivist assessment* (pp. 31–57). Newbury Park, CA: Sage.

Lyddon, W. J., & McLaughlin, J. T. (1992). Constructivist psychology: A heuristic framework. *The Journal of Mind and Behavior, 13*(1), 89–107.

Lyddon, W. J., & Satterfield, W. A. (1994). Relation of client attachment to therapist first- and second-order change assessments. *Journal of Cognitive Psychotherapy: An International Quarterly, 8,* 233–242.

Lyddon, W. J., & Sherry, A. (2001). Developmental personality styles: An attachment theory conceptualization of personality disorders. *Journal of Counseling and Development, 79,* 405–414.

Mahoney, M. J. (1984). Behaviorism and Individual Psychology: Contacts, conflicts, and future directions. In T. Reineit, Z. Otalora, & H. Kappus (Eds.), *Contacts of individual psychology with other forms of therapy* (pp. 70–82). Munich: Ernst Reinhardt Verlag.

Mahoney, M. J. (1985). Psychotherapy and human change processes. In M. J. Mahoney & A. Freeman (Eds.), *Cognition and psychotherapy* (pp. 3–48). New York: Plenum.

Mahoney, M. J. (1988a). Constructive metatheory: I. Basic features and historical foundations. *International Journal of Personal Construct Psychology, 1,* 1–35.

Mahoney, M. J. (1988b). Constructive metatheory: II. Implications for psychotherapy. *International Journal of Personal Construct Psychology, 1,* 299–315.

Mahoney, M. J. (1991). *Human change processes.* Delran, NJ: Basic.

Mahoney, M. J., & Lyddon, W. J. (1988). Recent developments in cognitive approaches to counseling and psychotherapy. *The Counseling Psychologist, 16,* 190–234.

Mair, M. (1988). Psychology and storytelling. *International Journal of Personal Construct Psychology, 1,* 125–137.
Mair, M. (1989). Kelly, Bannister, and a storytelling psychology. *International Journal of Personal Construct Psychology, 2,* 1–14.
Mair, M. (1990). Telling psychological tales. *International Journal of Personal Construct Psychology, 3,* 121–135.
Manaster, G., & Corsini, R. J. (1982). *Individual Psychology: Theory and practice.* Itasca, IL: Peacock.
Master, S. (1991). Constructivism and the creative power of the self. *Individual Psychology, 47,* 447–455.
Mosak, H. (1989). Adlerian psychotherapy. In R. J. Corsini & D. Wedding (Eds.), *Current psychotherapies* (4th ed., pp. 65–116). Itasca, IL: Peacock.
Neimeyer, G. J. (Ed.). (1993). *Constructivist assessment: A casebook.* Newbury Park, CA: Sage.
Neimeyer, R. A. (1994). The role of client-generated narratives in psychotherapy. *Journal of Constructivist Psychology, 7,* 229–242.
Neimeyer, R. A. (1995). An appraisal of constructivist psychotherapies. In M. J. Mahoney (Ed.), *Cognitive and constructive psychotherapies* (pp. 163–194). New York: Springer.
Nietzsche, F. (1967). *The will to power* (W. Kaufmann & R. J. Hollingdale, Trans.). New York: Vintage. (Original work published 1911)
Polanyi, M. (1967). *The tacit dimension.* Garden City, NY: Doubleday.
Popper, K. (1983). *Realism and the aim of science.* Totowa, NJ: Rowman & Littlefield.
Popper, K. (1987). Natural selection and the emergence of mind. In G. Radnitzky & W. W. Bartley III (Eds.), *Evolutionary epistemology, rationality, and the sociology of knowledge* (pp. 139–156). La Salle, IL: Open Court.
Popper, K., & Eccles, J. (1977). *The self and its brain.* New York: Routledge.
Russel, R. L. (1991). Narrative, cognitive representations, and change: New directions in cognitive theory and therapy. *Journal of Cognitive Psychotherapy, 5,* 239–256.
Safran, J. D. (1984a). Some implications of Sullivan's interpersonal theory for cognitive therapy. In M. Reda & M. J. Mahoney (Eds.), *Cognitive psychotherapies: Recent developments in theory, research, and practice* (pp. 251–272). Cambridge, MA: Ballinger.
Safran, J. D. (1984b). Assessing the cognitive interpersonal cycle. *Cognitive Therapy and Research, 8,* 333–348.
Safran, J. D. (1990a). Towards a refinement of cognitive therapy in light of interpersonal theory I: Theory. *Clinical Psychological Review, 10,* 87–105.
Safran, J. D. (1990b). Towards a refinement of cognitive therapy in light of interpersonal theory: II. Practice. *Clinical Psychological Review, 10,* 107–121.
Safran, J. D., & Segal, Z. V. (1990). *Interpersonal process in cognitive therapy.* New York: Praeger.
Safran, J. D., Vallis, T. M., Segal, Z. V., & Shaw, B. F. (1986). Assessment of core processes in cognitive therapy. *Cognitive Therapy and Research, 10,* 509–526.
Sarbin, T. R. (Ed.). (1986). *Narrative psychology: The storied nature of human conduct.* New York: Praeger.

Satterfield, W. A., & Lyddon, W. J. (1998). Client attachment and the working alliance. *The Counseling Psychology Quarterly, 11,* 407–415.

Schreiber, R., & Lyddon, W. J. (1998). Parental bonding and current psychological functioning among childhood sexual abuse survivors. *Journal of Counseling Psychology, 45,* 358–362.

Scott, C. N., Kelly, D., & Brandon, T. L. (1995). Realism, constructivism, and the Individual Psychology of Alfred Adler. *Individual Psychology, 51,* 4–20.

Shulman, B. H. (1985). Cognitive therapy and the Individual Psychology of Alfred Adler. In M. J. Mahoney & A. Freeman (Eds.), *Cognition and psychotherapy* (pp. 46–62). New York: Plenum.

Sullivan, H. S. (1953). *The interpersonal theory of psychiatry.* New York: Norton.

Sweeney, T. J. (1989). *Adlerian counseling: A practical approach for a new decade.* Muncie, IN: Accelerated Development.

Vaihinger, H. (1924). *The philosophy of 'as if'.* Berlin: Reuther & Reichard. (Original work published 1911)

Vallis, T. M. (1991). Theoretical and conceptual bases of cognitive therapy. In T. M. Vallis, J. L. Howes, & P. C. Miller (Eds.), *The challenge of cognitive therapy: Applications to nontraditional populations* (pp. 3–24). New York: Plenum.

van den Broek, P., & Thurlow, R. (1991). The role and structure of personal narratives. *Journal of Cognitive Psychotherapy, 5,* 257–274.

Vogel, D. (1994). Narrative perspectives in theory and therapy. *Journal of Constructivist Psychology, 7,* 243–261.

Weimer, W. B. (1977). A conceptual framework for cognitive psychology: Motor theories of the mind. In R. Shaw & J. D. Bransford (Eds.), *Perceiving, acting, and knowing: Toward an ecological psychology* (pp. 267–311). Hillsdale, NJ: Erlbaum.

White, M., & Epston, D. (1990). *Narrative means to therapeutic ends.* New York: Norton.

Part 2
Adlerian and Cognitive Psychotherapies

4

Commonalities Between Adlerian Psychotherapy and Cognitive Therapies: An Adlerian Perspective

Len Sperry

At the onset of this new millennium, it appears that cognitive and cognitive-behavioral therapies (CBTs) remain the dominant clinical approaches. Previously, that distinction was held by psychoanalytic approaches, at least until around the early 1960s, then by the humanistic psychotherapies through the early 1980s. Since the mid-1980s, cognitive therapy and related cognitive-behavioral approaches to psychotherapy have significantly influenced research, training, and clinical practice. For the past decade, grant applications to the National Institute of Mental Health (NIMH) for controlled-trial drug studies require that at least one arm of the proposed study involve a CBT comparison group. Guidelines for graduate training programs in counseling, clinical and counseling psychology, and even psychiatry, require that students receive training in CBT. Managed behavioral health organizations routinely adopt clinical practice guidelines that favor cognitive-behavioral interventions.

Furthermore, surveys of clinicians in the past decade typically report that the majority of clinicians identify their primary theoretical orientation as cognitive-behavioral. A recently published survey study showed that 38% of clinical psychologists and 30% of counseling psychologists reported their primary orientation as cognitive-behavioral; 99% of both clinical and counseling psychologists reported their primary orientation as integrative (Bechtoldt, Norcross, Wyckoff, Pokrywa, & Campbell, 2001).

Since the Adlerian psychotherapy orientation was not an option, one wonders which orientation adherents of the Adlerian orientation did endorse for this survey. Did they endorse the integrative, cognitive-behavioral, humanistic, existential, psychodynamic, systems, or "other" orientations? The Adlerian orientation has been conceptualized as a broader and more inclusive orientation than other formal theoretical orientations. For instance, Mosak and Maniacci (1999) emphasize its psychodynamic, cognitive, and behavioral dimensions; Dinkmeyer and Sperry (2000) emphasize its psychodynamic, cognitive-behavioral, systems, and humanistic (i.e., experiential and existential) dimensions. Thus, although the Adlerian orientation is broader than the cognitive-behavioral orientation, there is, nevertheless, considerable commonality between these two orientations or approaches.

Today, there is increasing interest in emphasizing commonalities and converging themes among therapeutic approaches. Several laudatory efforts to clarify theoretical and methodological commonalities have been reported (Goldfried & Castonguary, 1992; Miller, Hubble, & Duncan, 1997; Norcross & Goldfried, 1992). The purpose of this chapter is threefold: first, to identify and articulate several common themes in both Adlerian psychotherapy and the cognitive therapies; second, to suggest ways in which the cognitive therapies can enhance Adlerian psychotherapy; and third, to suggest ways in which Adlerian psychotherapy can enhance the cognitive therapies. Before proceeding with these tasks, it might be useful to set the stage for this discussion.

In his history of psychotherapy, Ellenberger (1970) suggests that the concepts and methods of many psychotherapy systems, including the cognitive therapies, overlap considerably with Adlerian psychotherapy. Ellenberger describes "two basic attitudes of human mind" (p. 648) that characterize all psychotherapy systems: Freud's system reflects the underlying nonrational philosophy of mind inherent in epicurianism and Romanticism; Adler's system reflects the underlying rational philosophy of mind inherent in stoicism and the Enlightenment. Clearly, Beck's cognitive therapy and other cognitive therapies reflect a rational philosophy of mind, and are, thus, more akin to Adlerian than Freudian assumptions and premises about human nature, psychopathology, and psychotherapy. The cognitive dimension of Adlerian psychology has been elegantly articulated by Forgus and Shulman (1979); the cognitive dimension of cognitive therapies has been articulated by several writers (e.g., Beck, 1964; Beck & Weishar, 1989; Ellis, 1962; Schwartz, 1988). Granted that Adlerian psychotherapy represents more than a cognitive approach—in that it is also a psychodynamic, a humanistic, and a systems theory—this discussion emphasizes its cognitive dimension.

SIMILARITIES BETWEEN ADLERIAN PSYCHOTHERAPY AND THE COGNITIVE THERAPIES

There are at least three basic constructs in Adlerian psychotherapy that are generally recognizable in the CBTs, and specifically in cognitive therapy. The three basic constructs are therapeutic focus, or the centrality of the lifestyle and lifestyle convictions as the focus of psychotherapy; therapeutic relationship, or the cooperative and collaborative nature of the client–therapist relationship; and therapeutic change, or the process of reeducation and reorientation (Dinkmeyer & Sperry, 2000; Sperry, 1992).

Therapeutic Focus

The individual's *lifestyle convictions* are the main therapeutic focus of Adlerian psychotherapy. Lifestyle convictions comprise the cognitive organization of the individual and can be described in terms of convictions about self, the world, the self-ideal, and ethical convictions (Mosak, 1989). Beck and Freeman (1990) note that the term *schema* can be traced to Bartlett (1932), but Adler actually used the term earlier. Adler, in his book *The Science of Living* (1929), described *schema of apperception* to refer to the individual's view of self and the world. Psychopathology, for Adler, reflected the individual's "neurotic schema" (Adler, 1956, p. 333). Kelly (1955) coined the term *personal constructs* to describe a similar phenomenon. Essentially, schemas reflect lifestyle convictions. Accordingly, schema and lifestyle convictions are used synonymously in this chapter.

Beck and his coworkers have elaborated schema theory within the cognitive perspective (Beck, 1964; Beck & Freeman, 1990). Beck and Freeman (1990) note that cognitive therapists focus on the dual levels of symptom structure (manifest problems) and underlying schema (inferred structures). Beck and his associates have described various types of schemas: cognitive, affective, motivational, instrumental, and control. Most well-developed, however, are the cognitive schemas concerning self-evaluation and worldview or evaluation of others. Some cognitive therapists (Young, 1990) have described early maladaptive schemas and triggering schemas that are strikingly similar to Adlerian formulations of various personality disorders.

Recently, the use of the terms *schema* and *schema theory* has emerged as central in the various subdisciplines of cognitive science, as well as by various psychotherapy schools (Stein, 1992). Advances in the cognitive neurosciences have offered considerable confirmation to the basic theoretical premises of both Adlerian psychotherapy and the cognitive therapies, particularly in the area of schemas (Gazzaniga, 1988; Stein & Young, 1992). Finally, research on narrative analysis (Oatley, 1992) and metaphor (Kopp, 1995) offer further validation of lifestyle convictions and schemas as the basis for understanding and changing an individual's maladaptive patterns.

Therapeutic Relationship

The current attention accorded collaboration and mutuality between therapist and client is a recent development in most psychotherapy systems. Previously, the therapist's role was understood as that of a superior, being both expert and healer, while the client's role was that of an inferior, being the learner and one in need of healing. Today, these roles tend to be described more in terms of equality, wherein client and therapist are fellow travelers on life's journey. Some 60 years ago, Adler stated that psychotherapy was essentially an exercise of cooperation. He noted that treatment failure always involved a lack of cooperation between client and therapist:

> Therefore, cooperation between patient and consultant, as the first, serious scientifically conducted attempt to raise social interest, is of paramount importance, and from the start, all measures should be taken to promote the cooperation of the patient with the consultant. (Adler, 1956, pp. 340–341)

Mosak (1989) states that, for the Adlerian, "a good therapeutic relationship is a friendly one, between equals" (p. 84).

Perhaps the most convincing of the contemporary proponents of collaboration is Beck. He uses the term *collaborative empiricism* to refer to a therapeutic relationship that is "collaborative and requires jointly determining the goals for treatment... and where the therapist and patient become co-investigators" (Beck & Weishaar, 1989, p. 301). Beck also believes that the therapist's role is that of a guide and catalyst who promotes corrective experiences in addition to utilizing warmth, accurate empathy, and genuineness to appreciate the client's personal worldview (Beck & Weishaar, 1989).

Several other cognitive-behavioral therapists also endorse the collaborative perspective (Schwartz, 1988; Woolford, 1988; Fishman, 1988). Turk and Meichenbaum (1983) accentuate the clinical value of a collaborative relationship when they advocate the importance of "entering the patient's perspective." In so doing, "the patient and therapist can work together to establish a similar understanding and common expectations (of treatment)" (p. 7).

Therapeutic Change

Therapeutic focus answers the "what" question, and therapeutic relationship answers the "who" question; therapeutic process answers the "how" question. More specifically, *therapeutic change* refers to the mechanisms of change that underlie the psychotherapeutic process. Adler taught that neurotic symptoms served the purpose of safeguarding the client's self-esteem (Adler, 1956). Freud originally conceived of ego defense mechanisms as "protection of the ego against instinctual demands" (Freud, 1936, p. 157). As the term *ego defense mechanism* is used today, it refers to the safeguarding of the self from outside threats. Adler believed that uncovering this neurotic safeguarding was the most important component of psychotherapy. He noted that this uncovering process takes place in a step-by-step, incremental fashion, through encouragement, reeducation, and reorientation. Beitman and Mooney (1991) argue that *desensitization* is the common mechanism for change in psychotherapy. Desensitization is a process of extinguishing an emotional response, such as anxiety, dysphoria, guilt, and so on, to a stimuli that formerly induced it.

Wolpe (1983) describes systematic desensitization as a step-by-step procedure for replacing anxiety with relaxation, while gradually increasing the client's exposure to an anxiety-producing situation or object. Thus, exposure, in varying degrees, leads to or produces desensitization. These various exposure treatments range from desensitization in fantasy to desensitization in vivo, and from implosion or flooding in fantasy to real-life flooding, modeling, operant conditioning, and cognitive rehearsal. In the process, desensitization and extinction clients must redeploy their attention away from negative self-evaluations and toward either the feared object itself or helpful environmental aspects. As a result, they learn a greater degree of self-control or mastery (Beitman & Mooney, 1991). Similarly, more cognitively oriented therapy approaches, such as cognitive therapy and rational-emotive therapy, target cognition to be desensitized through cognitive restructuring or disputation.

WHAT COGNITIVE THERAPY HAS TO OFFER ADLERIAN PSYCHOTHERAPISTS

I believe the cognitive therapies have much to offer the Adlerian psychotherapist, specifically in three areas: treatment strategies and techniques, specific treatment protocols, and combined treatment involving medication. The developers and extenders of the cognitive therapies have been notably prolific in developing and adapting a number of treatment strategies and tactics that could easily enhance the practice of more traditionally trained Adlerian psychotherapists.

For several decades, Adlerian psychotherapists have distinguished themselves from other dynamic therapists by their utilization of a wide array of treatment techniques and tactics, ranging from paradoxical injunctions to the use of fables and metaphor, in addition to the traditional methods of clarification, confrontation, and interpretation (Kopp, 1995; Mosak, 1989). For instance, 10 specific treatment strategies developed by Adlerians are described in *Adlerian Counseling and Psychotherapy* (Dinkmeyer, Dinkmeyer, & Sperry, 1987).

For more than a decade, cognitively oriented therapists have developed or adapted scores of treatment strategies and tactics. For example, McMullen (1986) has catalogued 80 techniques useful in the practice of cognitively oriented psychotherapy, in his *Handbook of Cognitive Therapy Techniques*. *Cognitive shift* is a central strategy in Beck's cognitive therapy, but several specific treatment techniques have been "designed to shift information processing" (Beck & Weishaar, 1989, p. 286). Twenty general treatment techniques, commonly utilizing cognitive therapy, are noted by Dattilio and Freeman (1992); more than 10 techniques specific to the treatment of personality disorders have been described (Beck & Freeman, 1990).

The cognitive therapies have also developed a number of specific protocols for various psychiatric disorders. Book-long treatises have been published on the treatment of personality disorders (Beck & Freeman, 1990), anxiety disorders (Beck & Emery, 1985), depression (Beck, Rush, Shaw, & Emery, 1979), borderline personality disorder (Layden, Newman, Freeman, & Morse, 1993), and marital conflict (Beck, 1988), to name a few. Several casebooks illustrating these treatment protocols are also available (i.e., Freeman & Dattilio, 1992). Adlerians can learn much from these protocols. They may even be disposed to articulate and disseminate, much more widely, their own protocols.

Furthermore, the cognitive therapies, particularly Beck's cognitive therapy, have been utilized in combination with other treatment modalities, particularly medication. The well-known NIMH Treatment of Depression Collaborative Research Program (TDCRP) (Elkin, 1994) further accentuated cognitive therapy's value as an effective treatment. TDCRP compared cognitive therapy to another form of psychotherapy, alone and in combination with an antidepressant. TDCRP and several other studies comparing cognitive therapy with medication, or in combination with medication, have effectively discounted the early claim of dynamic therapists that medication was contraindicated in psychotherapy, since it reduced the client's motivation for change. Unfortunately, a number of Adlerian psychotherapists continue to subscribe to this view. I believe that the overwhelming research data, indicating that medication can have a synergistic effect when combined with psychotherapeutic treatment, for certain types of depression and anxiety disorders, could be quite useful to Adlerian psychotherapists dealing with complex cases.

Finally, I believe that the cognitive therapies offer an important challenge—albeit an implicit challenge—to Adlerian psychotherapy. The challenge is to become more mainstream. Adlerian psychotherapy has been relatively content to rest on its historical laurels. Clearly, the cognitive and CBTs have assumed the status once accorded to psychoanalysis and other dynamic therapies. These newer treatments have become the gold standard of treatment today. Because Adlerian psychotherapy is an important forerunner of the cognitive therapies, Adlerians can, if they choose, become more active and public in articulating their theory and methods, knowing that they are very much part of the cognitive revolution.

WHAT ADLERIAN PSYCHOTHERAPY HAS TO OFFER COGNITIVE THERAPISTS

In my opinion, Adlerian psychotherapy and Adlerian psychology have three specific gifts to offer the cognitive therapies, that is, in addition to its birthright. These are a specific assessment method, an educational and value perspective, and a challenge to become more comprehensive and integrative.

The method utilized by Adlerian psychotherapists for eliciting, then formulating, lifestyle convictions is an Adlerian legacy that could be of considerable value to the cognitive therapist. The method originally described by Adler (1929) for eliciting early recollections (ERs) and the lifestyle is a relatively straightforward interview technique that is easily learned. Interview guides have been described by Powers and Griffith (1987) and Eckstein, Baruth, and Mahrer (1992), for developing competence in this technique. On the other hand, many of the methods utilized by cognitive therapists to elicit and formulate core maladaptive schemas are considerably more complex and reactive. For instance, Young (1990) notes that "eight steps are required to identify schemas" (p. 18). One of these steps is administering the Lazarus Multimodal Life History Questionnaire, as well as Young's Schema Questionnaire. Freeman (1992) describes a rather sophisticated method called the "critical incident technique," for both eliciting schemas and formulating or "developing a treatment conceptualization" (p. 13), as he calls it. This method appears to require considerable clinical sophistication on the part of the clinician. Kihlstrom and Cunningham (1991) have developed a computer program, called PERSPACE, to assess schemas of self and others. This program requires the client to respond to probe items, making it essentially a questionnaire.

Paper and pencil inventories, such as Young's Schema Questionnaire, are reactive assessment methods that invite measurement error, such as social desirability and instrument bias. On the other hand, the procedure for eliciting ERs is rather straightforward and considerably less reactive as an assessment method, since it is essentially a projective technique (Mosak, 1958). In short, the Adlerian approach to eliciting schemas seems to be quicker, more straightforward, and less reactive than methods described by cognitive therapists.

Central values of Adlerian psychology and psychotherapy are encouragement and democracy. An important concept, logical consequences, is related to both of these values. Adlerians have promulgated all three of these notions in their therapy, as well as in consultation and in education and psychoeducation. To my knowledge, cognitive therapies have yet to articulate an approach to parenting or to education. I suspect that these three concepts may be useful to our cognitive colleagues, whether in the therapeutic or psychoeducational contexts.

Finally, Adlerian psychotherapy can extend a challenge to its cognitive colleagues to become more comprehensive and integrative in their perspective. As a dynamic-humanistic-systemic-cognitive theory and treatment method, Adlerian psychotherapy is concerned with early life and systemic factors, including family, peer, and social dynamics (Sherman & Dinkmeyer, 1987). To date, there has been little recognition of early life determinants, including birth order, or environmental factors, such as family constellation, of personality in cognitive therapy. Beck posits that early negative experiences are the developmental precursors for global negative schemas regarding the self, current circumstances, and the future, but his theory is essentially an intrapsychic definition of psychopathology in which the role of the environment remains obscure. For Beck, "schemas are somehow non-representative of reality—they distort reality" (McCullough, 2000, p. 237). McCullough insists that negative schemas can also be representative constructions of actual environmental realities in a person's early life. Accordingly, "these earlier developmental perceptions of the individual's environment must become a central concern of the psychotherapists in assessing cognitive psychopathology in the present" (p. 237). On the other hand, the Adlerian view of psychopathology is broader and accounts for intrapsychic, interpersonal, and environmental factors.

As cognitive therapists become more involved with the treatment of the more severe personality disorders, they may find that a focus on dynamic and systemic issues may be helpful in both conceptualizing and treating the disorder. Currently, it seems that a focus on core maladaptive schemas is already deemed a necessity to the cognitive therapy of personality disorders (Beck & Freeman, 1990; Young, 1990). In a sense, this is cognitive therapy's first real foray into psychodynamics. However, there are other constructs that Adlerians have developed, such as psychological birth order, family constellation, and family atmosphere, which may offer considerable therapeutic leverage to cognitive therapists working with difficult clients. In short, Adlerians would challenge the cognitive therapies to become more than problem-solving approaches by integrating selective systemic and dynamic concepts.

CONCLUSION

In this chapter, three integral factors of Adlerian psychotherapy are noted to have a prominent place in the cognitive therapies, particularly the cognitive therapy of Beck and associates. They are: therapeutic focus, the client–therapist relationship, and strategy for therapeutic change. Several specific ways in which Adlerian and cognitive therapies can enhance, as well as challenge, each other are also described. Finally, it should also be noted that both approaches continue to benefit from developments in the field of cognitive neuroscience, which are confirming a number of theoretical premises of both approaches, most noticeably those about schemas and schema formation.

REFERENCES

Adler, A. (1929). *The science of living*. New York: Greenberg.
Adler, A. (1956). *The Individual Psychology of Alfred Adler* (H. Ansbacher & R. Ansbacher, Eds.). New York: Harper & Row.
Bartlett, F. (1932). *Remembering*. New York: Columbia University Press.
Bechtoldt, H., Norcross, J., Wyckoff, L., Pokrywa, L., & Campbell, L. (2001). Theoretical orientations and employments settings of clinical and counseling psychologists: A comparative study. *The Clinical Psychologist, 54*, 1, 3–6.
Beck, A. (1964). Thinking and depression: II. Theory and therapy. *Archives of General Psychiatry, 10*, 561–571.
Beck, A. (1988). *Love is never enough*. New York: Harper & Row.
Beck, A., & Emery, G. (1985). *Anxiety disorders and phobias: A cognitive perspective*. New York: Basic Books.
Beck, A., & Freeman, A. (1990). *Cognitive therapy of personality disorders*. New York: Guilford.
Beck, A., Rush, A., Shaw, B., & Emery, G. (1979). *Cognitive therapy of depression*. New York: Guilford.
Beck, A., & Weishaar, M. (1989). Cognitive therapy. In R. Corsini & D. Wedding (Eds.), *Current psychotherapies* (4th ed., pp. 285–322). Itasca, IL: Peacock.
Beitman, B., & Mooney, J. (1991). Exposure and desensitization as common change processes in pharmacotherapy and psychotherapy. In B. Beitman & G. Klerman (Eds.), *Integrating pharmacotherapy and psychotherapy* (pp. 435–445). Washington, DC: American Psychiatric Press.
Dattilio, F., & Freeman, A. (1992). Introduction to cognitive therapy. In A. Freeman & F. Dattilio (Eds.), *Comprehensive casebook of cognitive therapy* (pp. 3–12). New York: Plenum.
Dinkmeyer, D., Dinkmeyer, D., & Sperry, L. (1987). *Adlerian counseling and psychotherapy* (2nd ed.). Columbus, OH: Merrill.
Dinkmeyer, D., & Sperry, L. (2000). *Counseling and psychotherapy: An integrated, Individual Psychology approach* (3rd ed.). Upper Saddle, NJ: Merrill/Prentice Hall.
Eckstein, D., Baruth, L., & Mahrer, D. (1992). *Life-Style Assessment* (3rd ed.). Dubuque, IA: Kendall-Hunt.

Elkin, I. (1994). The NIMH treatment of depression collaboration research program. In A. Bergin & S. Garfield (Eds.), *Handbook of psychotherapy and behavior change* (4th ed., pp. 114–139). New York: Wiley.

Ellenberger, H. (1970). *The discovery of the unconscious: The history and evolution of dynamic psychiatry.* New York: Harper & Row.

Ellis, A. (1962). *Reason and emotion in psychotherapy.* Secaucus, NJ: Lyle Stuart.

Fishman, D. (1988) Paradigmatic decisions in behavior therapy: A provisional roadmap. In D. Fishman, C. Franks, & E. Rotgers (Eds.), *Paradigms in behavior therapy: Present and promise* (pp. 323–362). New York: Springer.

Forgus, R., & Shulman, B. (1979). *Personality: A cognitive view.* Englewood Cliffs, NJ: Prentice-Hall.

Freeman, A. (1992). The development of treatment conceptualizations in cognitive therapy. In A. Freeman & F. Dattilio (Eds.), *Comprehensive casebook of cognitive therapy* (pp. 13–23). New York: Plenum.

Freeman, A., & Dattilio, F. (Eds.). *Comprehensive casebook of cognitive therapy.* New York: Plenum.

Freud, A. (1936). *The ego and the mechanisms of defense.* New York: International Universities Press.

Gazzaniga, M. (1988). *Mind matters: How mind and body interact to create our conscious lives.* Boston: Houghton-Mifflin.

Goldfried, M., & Castonguay, L. (1992). The future of psychotherapy integration. *Psychotherapy: Theory, Research, Practice, Training, 29,* 4–10.

Kelly, G. (1955). *The psychology of personal constructs.* New York: Norton.

Kihlstrom, J., & Cunninghan, R. (1991). Mapping interpersonal space. In M. Horowitz (Ed.), *Person schemas and maladaptive interpersonal patterns* (pp. 331–338). Chicago: University of Chicago Press.

Kopp, P. (1995). *Metaphor therapy: Using client-generated metaphors in psychotherapy.* New York: Brunner/Mazel.

Layden, M., Newman, C., Freeman, A., & Morse, S. (1993). *Cognitive therapy of borderline personality disorder.* Boston: Allyn & Bacon.

McCullough, J. (2000). *Treatment for chronic depression: Cognitive behavioral analysis system of psychotherapy.* New York: Guilford.

McMullin, R. (1986). *Handbook of cognitive therapy techniques.* New York: Norton.

Miller, S., Hubble, M., & Duncan, B. (1997). *Escape from Babel: Toward a unifying language for psychotherapy practice.* New York: Norton.

Mosak, H. (1958). Early recollections as a projective technique. *Journal of Projective Techniques, 22,* 302–311.

Mosak, H. (1989). Adlerian psychotherapy. In R. Corsini & D. Wedding (Eds.), *Current psychotherapies* (4th ed., pp. 65–118). Itasca, IL: Peacock.

Mosak, H., & Maniacci, M. (1999). *Primer of Adlerian psychology. The analytic-behavioral-cognitive psychology of Alfred Adler.* New York: Bruner/Mazel.

Norcross, J., & Goldfried, M. (Eds.). (1992). *Handbook of psychotherapy integration.* New York: Basic Books.

Oatley, K. (1992). Integrative action of narrative. In D. Stein & J. Young (Eds.), *Cognitive science and clinical disorders* (pp. 151–170). San Diego, CA: Academic Press.

Powers, R., & Griffith, J. (1987). *Understanding life-style: The psycho-clarity process.* Chicago: The Americas Institute of Adlerian Studies.

Schwartz, G. (1988). From behavior therapy to cognitive behavior therapy to systems therapy: Toward an integrative health science. In D. Fishman, C. Franks, & E. Rotgers (Eds.), *Paradigms in behavior therapy: Present and promise* (pp. 294–320). New York: Springer.

Sherman, R., & Dinkmeyer, D. (1987). *Systems of family therapy: An Adlerian integration.* New York: Brunner/Mazel.

Sperry, L. (1992). Psychotherapy systems: An Adlerian integration with implications for older adults. *Individual Psychology, 48,* 451–461.

Stein, D. (1992). Schemas in the cognitive and clinical sciences: An integrative construct. *Journal of Psychotherapy Integration, 2,* 45–63.

Stein, D., & Young, J. (1992). Schema approach to personality disorders. In D. Stein & J. Young (Eds.), *Cognitive science and clinical disorders* (pp. 271–288). San Diego, CA: Academic Press.

Turk, D., & Meichenbaum, D. (1983). *Pain and behavioral medicine: A cognitive-behavioral approach.* New York: Guilford.

Wolpe, J. (1983). *The practice of behavior therapy* (3rd ed.). New York: Pergamon.

Woolford, R. (1988). The self in cognitive behavior therapy. In D. Fishman, C. Franks, & E. Rotgers (Eds.), *Paradigms in behavior therapy: Present and promise* (pp. 168–184). New York: Springer.

Young, J. (1990). *Cognitive therapy for personality disorders: A schema-focused approach.* Sarasota, FL: Professional Resource Exchange.

5

Adlerian Psychology and Cognitive-Behavioral Therapy: A Cognitive Therapy Perspective

Arthur Freeman and June Urschel

In the last several years, cognitive behavior therapy (CBT) has attracted increasing interest from mental health professionals around the world. The cognitive revolution discussed by Mahoney (1974) has matured so that the CBTs have moved from an area of fringe interest to the forefront of professional interest. Cognitive therapy has become a meeting ground for therapists from diverse theoretical and philosophical positions, ranging from the behavioral to the psychoanalytic. Psychodynamic therapists find in CBT a dynamic core that involves working to alter basic schemas. Adlerian therapists find in CBT a short-term, active, directive, collaborative, psychoeducational model of psychotherapy. Forgus and Shulman (1979) and Shulman (1985) state that, as Adler developed his theories of dysfunction and therapy, he introduced, "a number of cognitive concepts," thus placing him "securely among the cognitive personality theorists and cognitive therapists" (p. 244).

It is interesting to present Adlerian concepts to psychology students or to mental health professionals who have been trained in a CBT model. The responses can be categorized into three main types. The first type of response involves extensive note taking. To this group, the material is new, interesting, useful, and relevant. The second type of response is manifested by those who sit back and simply nod. After all, these ideas make sense and appear to be consistent with CBT. What's new? A third response involves a mild protest. After all, who is this Adler fellow to co-opt so many of the CBT ideas?

Kurt Adler (personal communication, 1983) called cognitive therapy "a most reasonable extension of my father's work." Eva Dreikurs Ferguson (personal communication, 1990), a well-known Adlerian psychologist, whose father, Rudolf Dreikurs, was a coworker with Alfred Adler and one of the major theoreticians and teachers in Adlerian psychology (AP), in commenting on a presentation of the basic theory and techniques of cognitive therapy, stated, "Nothing (was said) with which my father would disagree."

From the CBT side, Beck, Rush, Shaw, and Emery (1979), Ellis (1985, 1989), and Freeman, Pretzer, Fleming, and Simon (1990) all credit their CBT work to an early grounding in AP. Dowd and Kelly (1980), in their seminal paper, conclude, "Perhaps Cognitive-Behavioral Psychology's strong array of treatment and research strategies could be joined with the theoretical concepts of Adlerian Psychology to the benefit of both of these systems" (p. 134).

We have three goals in this chapter. First, we describe and discuss the similarities and differences in the conceptualization, theory, and practices between cognitive therapy and Adlerian therapy. Our second goal is to describe and discuss the importance of an Adlerian approach to cognitive therapists and how cognitive therapists can profit from a thorough understanding of Adlerian psychology and psychotherapy. Third, we identify the basic CBT treatment focus and techniques that we believe to be of value to Adlerian therapy.

SIMILARITIES BETWEEN COGNITIVE THERAPY AND ADLERIAN THERAPY

Although most often grouped among psychoanalysts, Adler found purely motivational theories of behavior insufficient to explain human behavior. His work focused on understanding the beliefs and convictions that a person developed. These beliefs were part of what became the *lifestyle*. The apperceptive schema or personal rules of life direct the individual's movement through life. In considering the structure of a personality, the chief difficulty is that its unity, its particular style of life and goal, is not built upon objective reality, but upon the subjective view the individual takes of the facts of life (Ansbacher & Ansbacher, 1956).

One of the basic Adlerian constructs is the style of life. Although used as a generic term, one might make a distinction between the notions of *schema* and *style of life*. According to Ansbacher and Ansbacher (1956),

> The former belongs to the perceptual and ideational area, as the equivalent of the individual's opinion of or view of himself and the world, while the style of life, as the individual's consistent movement toward his goal, is the behavioral counterpart. (p. 184)

It is necessary for the client and for the therapist to understand the schema, not as end points, but as part of the process and the subscript that generates the cognitive errors or distortions. The lifestyle and its component schema are acquired early in life. The ability to modify or reinterpret the schema is based on how compelling they are, and on the source of the schema. In many cases, they are learned from a powerful and credible source and will resist change.

The similarities between CBT and AP are rooted in this shared conceptual framework of examining the rules of life that each person acquires. The greatest differences between the treatment models rest in the strategic and technical implementation of the therapies. CBT, like Adlerian therapy, is a dynamic therapy (Freeman, Simon, Pretzer, & Fleming, 1990). The focus is on helping the client listen to and understand their thinking, and to then appraise how the thinking is influenced by personal, cultural, religious, age-related, gender, and social schema. According to Mosak (1995), "Understanding the individual requires understanding his or her cognitive organization and life-style. Schema develop early in life to help to organize experience, to understand it, to predict it, and to control it" (p. 52). Shulman (1985) states, "Apperceptive schema grow in number and finally require integration into a master plan so that action in the world does not lose sight of the guiding idealized fiction" (p. 246). According to Adler, "The uncovering of the . . . style of life for the client is the most important component in therapy" (Ansbacher & Ansbacher, 1956, p. 334).

A schema that is strongly held, and is seen to be essential for the person's safety, well-being, or existence, will be more powerful as a directing force within the person's life. If the schema was adopted and internalized early in life and was powerfully reinforced by significant others, it will similarly be more present in the personality style (Beck, Freeman, and Associates, 1990). If the schema was acquired prior to the acquisition of language (i.e., during the sensorimotor stage), the schema will be very powerful and direct behavior, although the individual may not be able to identify the source of the schema. It appears to come from out of a fog (Layden, Newman, Freeman, & Morse, 1993).

Schema are in a constant state of change and evolution. From the child's earliest years, there is a need to alter old schema and develop new schema, to meet the different and increasingly complex demands of the world (*adaptation*). The infant's conception of reality is governed by their limited interaction with their world, so the infant may initially perceive the entire world as their crib and the few caretakers that care for and comfort it. As the infant develops additional skills of mobility and interaction (*compensation*), the schema are altered by the new data. Environmental data and experience are only taken in by individuals as they can utilize this data in terms of their own subjective experiences. The schema are self-selective, in that individuals may ignore certain environmental stimuli that they were not able to integrate or synthesize. There is an active and evolutionary process in which all perceptions and cognitive structures are applied to new functions (*assimilation*), while new cognitive structures are developed to serve old functions in new situations (*accommodation*) (Rosen, 1985, 1989). Some individuals may persist in utilizing old structures, without fitting them to the new circumstances in which they are involved, but using them completely without measuring fit or appropriateness. They may further fail to accommodate or build new structures. This behavior would generally be maladaptive.

The element common in both the AP and CBT models is helping clients to examine the manner in which they construe and understand the world (cognitions) and to experiment with new ways of responding (behavioral). By learning to understand the idiosyncratic way in which they perceive self, world, and experience, and the prospects for the future, clients can be helped to alter negative affect, change their view of our life experience, and to behave more adaptively.

Based on their schema, individuals can distort in a variety of positive or negative ways. Clients who distort in a positive direction may be the "fool that rushes in where angels fear to tread" and may view life in an unrealistically positive way. They may take chances that most people would avoid, that is, starting a new business or investing in a risky new stock. If successful, the positive distorter is vindicated and may be envied for their courage. If unsuccessful, positive distorters may see their failure as a consequence of taking a low-yield chance.

However, it is the negative distortions or maladaptive thoughts (automatic thoughts) that generally become the focus of therapy. The therapist works to make the distortions manifest in content, degree of client belief, and style, and to help to identify the impact of the distortions on the client's life. The distortions are the thematic directional signs that point to, or suggest, the underlying schema. The distortions occur in many combinations and permutations, and are essentially "normal." When these distortions become exaggerated and a source of discomfort or dysfunction, the client will generally seek help. Often, these distortions are parenthetic statements to what the client is saying. For example, when the client says, "I'll be embarrassed," then has a strong emotional reaction to the notion of embarrassment, the parenthetic or unspoken part of the statement might be, " . . . and that would be terrible/ awful" or " . . . and I won't survive the embarrassment," or " . . . and it will serve me right for thinking I could do that." Certain types or combinations of distortions have become emblematic of particular styles of behaving or of certain clinical syndromes.

Many clients have difficulty in dealing or coping with internal or external stimuli, because of a lack of basic skills. These skill deficits might be narrow and cause difficulty in small, isolated areas, but they may also be broad deficits and include difficulty or inability to respond to depressogenic or anxiogenic thoughts. In addition, social skills deficits make it difficult to cope in social situations or to recognize the beginnings of a panic attack and to then take the appropriate action. As individuals develop skills to manage their difficulties, they are also in a position to transmute the private logic upon which their lifestyle is based.

The four goals of both CBT and Adlerian therapy consist of establishing a collaborative and cooperative relationship; uncovering the client's private logic and core schema that define life goals; helping the client to recognize the above and increase his or her understanding of self; and reorienting the client, through the development of alternative cognitive and behavioral skills, to establish more adaptive life goals. The major goal of CBT is to increase clients' skills, so that they can more effectively deal with the exigencies of life, and thereby have a greater sense of control and self-efficacy in their lives (Bandura, 1977).

CONTRIBUTIONS OF ADLERIAN PSYCHOLOGY TO CBT

Techniques

Two specific AP techniques that are useful for CBT are the use of the individual's early recollections (ERs) (Adler, 1937; Lingg & Kottman,

1991; Manaster & Corsini, 1982) and the use of dreams (Freeman & Boyll, 1992). The focus of both dreams and ERs is on their manifest content. They both reveal important aspects of the individual's current perception of life. ERs contain the basic mistakes of the individual, which are the individual's faulty assumptions about self, others, and the world, a notion used by Beck et al. (1979) and labeled the *cognitive triad*. Lingg and Kottman (1991) describe how these assumptions govern behavior and how the individual may not necessarily be aware of them. By asking the client for their earliest recollection, the therapist obtains a sample of images that are important and powerful for that client. Accordingly, an individual selects from his past those events, real or fantasized, which have a bearing on his current situation. Adler believed that the earliest memory is of particular relevance in depicting one's fundamental attitude toward life (Bruhn & Last, 1982). Through the disclosure of early memories, the individual shows the therapist those themes that reveal the core schema that motivate the individual to make certain choices and rule out others and can help to uncover the individual's private logic or idiosyncratic meaning given to events in life. According to the cognitive-perceptual model (Bruhn, 1990), an individual's frame of reference is born out of the first perceptual process that integrates his or her needs, fears, interests, and major beliefs. The usefulness in interpretation of ERs is in the possibility of developing an alternative meaning and modifying the existing schema.

One of the aims of the therapist is to assist the individual in modifying those aspects of personality that generate problematic or self-defeating responses to living. Memories from early childhood reveal an individual's central tendency of movement and the consistency of this movement with the individual's personality. This is essential in developing effective therapeutic interventions and treatment goals with the client. Treatment goals often target dysfunctional automatic thoughts and errors in cognition.

Dreams also offer ways of better understanding the client's cognitive content and set. The following guidelines can be set for CBT dream work:

1. The dream needs to be understood in thematic rather than symbolic terms.
2. The thematic content of the dream is idiosyncratic to the dreamer and must be viewed within the context of the dreamer's life.

3. The specific language and images of the dream are important and must be questioned for idiosyncratic meaning.
4. The affective responses to the dreams can be seen as similar to the dreamer's affective response in waking situations.
5. The particular length of the dream is of lesser import than the content.
6. The dream is a product of, and the responsibility of, the dreamer.
7. Dream material is amenable to the same cognitive restructuring as any automatic thoughts.
8. Dreams can be used when the client appears "stuck" in therapy.
9. Dreams cannot become the sole focus of the session and need to be dealt with as part of the agenda.
10. Imagery associated with the dreams can be quite useful in the therapeutic work.

Social Interest

Adlerian psychotherapy is rooted in the premise that the individual is embedded in the social context in which one is raised and lives. Difficulties are typically viewed as social problems, that is, problems of interaction with others, involving humankind's interconnectedness. The therapist never focuses on an isolated human being, but rather on the various aspects of the social system. These cognitions and behaviors are often accompanied with negative social and/or interpersonal consequences. It seems necessary, therefore, for the cognitive therapist to theoretically include this process of social interest. Social interest is contained in cooperation, interpersonal and social relations, identification with one's group, and empathy (Hall & Lindzey, 1970).

Adler asserted that the first possibility for social interest, and the building of the attendant social schema, is in the relationship between mother and child (Ansbacher & Ansbacher, 1956). A second feature of social interest is that of cooperation. Initially, cooperation is experienced in the relationship between the infant and primary caregiver (attachment) and continues as the child extends himself or herself beyond this relationship (Hall & Lindzey, 1970). Ideally, the infant who is fortified with the realization of his or her primary caregiver's dependability, availability, warmth, and sensitivity will be more inclined to go forth and engage the environment. Lacking this realization, the child may develop schema relative to danger and exhibit insecurity and an abatement of exploratory behavior (Newman & Newman, 1995).

As social interest develops, it is expressed through empathy and identification with the family, peers, and the larger community. Social feeling can best be defined as the ability to take the perspective of others, that is, to "see with the eyes of another, to hear with the ears of another, to feel with the heart of another" (Adler, 1964, p. 42). With social interest present, the individual will have an understanding that both the comforts and discomforts of life are a part of living (Adler, 1964).

CONTRIBUTIONS OF CBT TO ADLERIAN THERAPY

Therapeutic Structure

The CBT model offers a high degree of structure that helps the client make best use of the therapy experience. The therapist takes a directive role in the treatment conceptualization, collaboration, and planning. Interpretations are avoided in favor of Socratic questioning. This avoids increasing the client's sense of inferiority (i.e., the therapist knows what is really wrong with me), which decreases the client's self-efficacy. The Socratic questioning develops greater awareness in the client. The therapist must plan and develop hypotheses about what reinforces and maintains dysfunctional thinking and behavior. Further, the therapist can offer hypotheses for consideration, act as a resource person, or directly point out areas of difficulty.

The client must be an active participant in the therapeutic process. This implies that the client has made a decision and commitment to try to change, without which therapy will be difficult, if not impossible.

Therapists must be able to generate a collaborative set, so that clients see themselves as partners in the process, not merely as subjects to be "therapized" or "worked on." The collaboration may not always be equally shared, but may be divided 30–70, or 70–30, with the therapist providing most of the energy or work within a particular session or in the therapy more generally. As the therapy progresses successfully, the proportion of client-to-therapist work would shift. The therapeutic goal is to help the client work to the limit of their ability.

Perhaps the most important elements are the structure, focus, and goal orientation of therapy. By avoiding the casual, free-associative meandering that has been so typical of most dynamic therapies, the therapist–client partnership can move quickly and directly into those areas that create the most difficulty.

The time-limited nature of CBT is not measured in the number of sessions, but rather in the manner in which the therapy is conducted. Therapy must have a beginning, middle, and an end. By setting near-point, midpoint, and far-point goals, the client's problem list can be dealt with in an ordered and reasonable fashion. Adler typically informed his clients that the therapy would take 8–10 weeks. Regarding the duration of therapy, he recommended that clients be told, "Let us begin. In a month I shall ask you whether we are on the right track. If not, we shall break it off" (Ansbacher & Ansbacher, 1964, p. 201).

The CBT work shifts from a symptom focus (i.e., the automatic thoughts) to a schema focus (i.e., the underlying dynamic core). A particular schema or schematic constellation may engender a great deal of emotion and be emotionally bound by the individual's past experience, by the sheer weight of the time for which that schema has been held, or by the relative importance and meaning of the individuals from whom the schema were acquired. The client can, with the proper training, describe schema in great detail. The therapist can also deduce the schema from behavior or automatic thoughts. Schema that are acquired very early in the developmental process, through sensorimotor channels, may be among the hardest to change, in that the therapist is attempting to change sensorimotor learning utilizing abstract formal operations techniques (Layden et al., 1993).

Finally, there is a behavioral component that involves the way the belief system governs the individual's responses to a particular stimulus or set of stimuli. In seeking to alter a particular schema that has endured for a long period of time, it would be necessary to help the individual address the belief from as many different perspectives as possible: cognitive, behavioral, situational, and affective. There cannot be a pure strategy that focuses on only one area, for example, expecting that a change in behavior will always bring about changes in cognition and affect. Significant others not only help to form the schema, but also help to maintain the particular schema, be they negative or positive. The long-standing nature of the schema is evident when clients describe themselves as displaying particular characteristics "as far back as I can remember."

The importance of the interpersonal process in CBT has been described and elucidated by Safran and Segal (1990). A full developmental, family, social, occupational, educational, medical, and psychiatric history is taken. This data is essential in helping to turn client complaints into a working problem list and to develop the treatment conceptualization. The establishment of a discrete problem list helps both client and therapist have an idea of where the therapy is going, a general time/energy framework, and to be able to assess therapeutic progress. Having established and agreed upon a problem list and focus for therapy, the individual sessions are then structured through agenda-setting.

Agenda-setting at the beginning of the session allows both client and therapist to put issues of concern on the agenda for the day, and allows the therapist to structure a session that is broad enough to use the available time without being so broad as to leave much of the agenda work incomplete. The agenda setting allows for continuity between sessions, so that sessions are not individual events, but rather part of a continuous whole. A typical agenda might include:

1. Rapport building
2. Review of any self-report scales
3. Setting the agenda
4. Overview of the client's week
5. Review of homework
6. Problems are listed in the agenda
7. Session review

This gives the therapist an opportunity to help the client to clarify the goals and accomplishments of the session. The homework for the next session can be emphasized and the session given closure. Finally, clients can be asked for their response to the session.

In CBT, a number of assessment tools are used as part of the ongoing data collection. These might include the Beck Depression Inventory-II (BDI-II) (Beck, Steer, & Brown, 1996). Weekly administration of the BDI-II, prior to each session, can serve to provide objective data about therapeutic progress, and as an aid in helping validate or challenge the client's assumptions about self, world, and the future. The BDI-II can be used as a homework form when clients report diurnal mood fluctuations.

When anxiety is a target symptom, the Beck Anxiety Inventory (BAI) (Beck, 1993a), a 21-item self-report symptom checklist designed to measure the severity of anxiety-related symptoms is useful. The BAI is diagnostic both quantitatively and qualitatively in a fashion similar to the BDI.

For clients who report suicidal thinking, the Beck Hopelessness Scale (Beck, 1993b), and the Beck Scale of Suicidal Ideation (Beck, 1991) are useful tools. Both measures may also be used as indexes of change. As the client learns new ways of coping, experiences greater self-efficacy, and perceives change, the level of hopelessness decreases.

Treatment Conceptualization

The treatment conceptualization will be based on family and developmental histories, test data, interview material, and reports of previous therapists or other professionals. This conceptualization must meet several criteria. It must be useful, simple, theoretically coherent, explain past behavior, make sense of present behavior, and able to predict future behavior. In developing the conceptualization, the following questions must be answered, to generate the most complete clinical picture of why this individual feels/thinks/behaves as he or she does.

- Is the client in real danger? If the client faces a validated threat or danger, all of the interpretation and reattribution will have a limited effect. The therapist must ascertain whether there is an accurate assessment of the facts and reality.
- What attribution does the client make about the responsibility and causation of their difficulty?
- Has the client made an accurate self-assessment? Clients will often have erroneous and distorted views of personal efficacy, skills, and strengths.
- What are the expectations that clients have governing their behavior and the behavior of others? Are the expectations for self (or therapist) within the bounds of probability? For example, the belief that they must change.
- What are the dysfunctional/distorted/automatic thoughts that are part of the day-to-day life of the client?
- What are the schema that are represented by the distortions, and how do the schema impact on the behaviors?
- What skills are needed to cope more effectively?
- What behavioral responses need to be modified to allow more effective coping?

Consideration of the above areas should help to guide the therapist toward a more systematic and effective intervention.

If a particular idea is only partially believed by the individual, it is much easier for them to give it up, compared to asking them to challenge what they see and regard as "self." Any challenge to the self needs to be the result of a careful, guided discovery based on collaboration, compared to a direct, confrontational, and disputational stance that will increase the client's anxiety.

Cognitive and Behavioral Techniques

Perhaps the major contribution of CBT to AP is the delineation of specific cognitive and behavioral techniques. These techniques are taught to clients to help them respond in more functional ways. The precise mix of cognitive and behavioral techniques will depend on the client's skills, the therapist's skills, the level of pathology, and the treatment goals. For the severely debilitated client, the initial goals of treatment would be focused on the client doing self-help tasks. Graded task assignments can be used with great success. Starting at the bottom of a hierarchy of difficulty, and moving through successively more difficult tasks, can help the client achieve a greater sense of personal efficacy. This personal efficacy can then be used as evidence for the cognitive work in therapy. Pharmacotherapy may be an essential ingredient in the therapy program developed for different clients.

By skillfully moving between various interventions, the therapist can teach clients specific intervention skills, so that clients can become their own therapist. Cognitive techniques include:

1. Idiosyncratic meaning. The client can be questioned directly on the meanings of their words and thoughts.
2. Questioning the evidence. What evidence is the client using to maintain and strengthen an idea or belief? Questioning the evidence also requires examining the sources of data.
3. Reattribution. The therapist can help the client to distribute responsibility among all relevant parties.
4. Examining options and alternatives. Helping the client to generate additional options.
5. Decatastrophizing. Reducing the catastrophic interpretation of a situation.

6. Fantasized consequences. Describing the fantasies and images regarding various concerns and anticipated consequences.
7. Advantages and disadvantages. Examining the advantages and the disadvantages of both sides of an issue.
8. Turning adversity to advantage. Turning a seeming disaster to advantage. This balancing puts the client's experience into a perspective.
9. Guided association/discovery. This therapist-guided technique involves the use of chained or guided association, using the Socratic questioning.
10. Use of exaggeration or paradox. By taking an idea to its extreme, the therapist can often help to move the family to a more central position vis-à-vis a particular belief.
11. Scaling. For those clients who see things as all or nothing, the technique of scaling experiences from a particular experience from 0 to 10, or seeing things as existing on a life-referenced continuum, is very important.
12. Externalization of voices. The client "hears" the dysfunctional voices in their head. By having the therapist take the part of the dysfunctional voice, the client can get practice in adaptive responding.
13. Self-instruction. Clients can be taught to offer direct self-instructions for more adaptive behavior or, in some cases, counterinstructions, to avoid dysfunctional behavior.
14. Thought-stopping. Dysfunctional thoughts often have a snowball effect for the individual. Thought-stopping is best used when the thoughts are about to start or just start, not in the middle of the process.
15. Distraction. Maintaining two thoughts at the same strength simultaneously is almost impossible. By having clients focus on complex counting, addition, or subtraction, they are rather easily distracted from other thoughts.
16. Direct disputation. There are times when direct disputation is helpful, especially when there is the imminence of a suicide attempt. They must be used carefully, judiciously, and with skill.
17. Labeling of distortions. The more that the therapist can do to identify the nature and content of the dysfunctional thinking, and to help label the types of distortions that clients utilize, the less frightening the entire process becomes.
18. Developing replacement imagery. Clients can be helped to develop coping images, for example, rather than imaging failure,

or recalling defeat or embarrassment, the therapist can practice with the client new, effective, coping images. Once well-practiced, clients can do image substitution.

The goals in using behavioral techniques within the context of CBT are manifold. The first goal is to utilize direct behavioral strategies and techniques to test dysfunctional thoughts and behaviors. By having the client try feared or avoided behaviors, data is collected and old ideas can be directly challenged. A second use of behavioral techniques is to practice new behaviors both in the office and at home.

1. Activity scheduling. For clients who are feeling overwhelmed, the activity schedule can be used to plan more effective time use. The activity schedule is both a retrospective tool to assess past time utilization and a prospective tool to help plan better time use.
2. Mastery and pleasure ratings. The activity schedule can also be used to assess and plan activities that offer clients both a sense of personal efficacy (mastery, 1–10), and pleasure (1–10). The greater the mastery and pleasure, the lower the rates of anxiety and depression.
3. Social skills or assertiveness training. If clients lack specific social skills, it is incumbent upon the therapist to either help them to gain the skills or to make a referral for skills training.
4. Bibliotherapy. Several excellent books can be assigned as readings for homework. A trip to the local bookstore's self-help section will net a number of books that can be targeted for particular problems.
5. Graded task assignments (GTA). GTAs involve a series of small sequential steps that lead to the desired goal. By setting out a task, then arranging the necessary steps in a hierarchy, clients can be helped to make reasonable progress with a minimum of stress.
6. Behavioral rehearsal/role-playing. The therapist can serve as teacher and guide, offering direct feedback on performance. The therapist can monitor the client's performance, offer suggestions for improvement, and model new behaviors, before the client attempts the behavior in vivo.
7. In vivo exposure. Although very time-intensive, the therapist can go with clients into feared situations. The in vivo exposure can

be part of the office-based therapy, along with the client-generated homework.
8. Relaxation training. Relaxation training can be taught in the office, then practiced by the client for homework.

The Daily Record of Dysfunctional Thoughts

One of the most powerful techniques in CBT involves helping the client to challenge dysfunctional thinking. The Daily Record of Dysfunctional Thoughts (DTR) is an ideal format for testing dysfunctional thoughts. The process begins with the client identifying the thought, the emotion, or the situation that causes them difficulty. If the client presents with an emotional issue (e.g., "I'm very sad"), the therapist needs to inquire as to the situations that might engender the emotion and the attendant thoughts. If the client presents with a thought (e.g., "I'm a loser"), the therapist needs to ascertain the feelings and the situation. Finally, the client may present a situation (e.g., "My husband left me"). The therapist needs to determine the thoughts and the emotions. Statements, such as "I feel like a loser," need to be reframed as thoughts, and the emotions that are a concomitant of the thought elicited. The following examples demonstrate the use of the DTR.

Often, clients phrase their thoughts as questions, for example, "Why does this always happen to me?" "Why can't I maintain a relationship?" or "Why doesn't my life turn out better?" A heuristic view is that questions are generally functional. It is important to ask questions, then to answer them. The dysfunctional thoughts are more generally declarative, rather than interrogatory (i.e., "This always happens to me," "I can't maintain a relationship," and "My life is less than I had hoped for"). The cognitive techniques can be used to question clients' conclusions, for example, the dysfunctional thought, "There's something terribly wrong with me."

No therapy takes place solely within the confines of the consulting room. It is important for the client to understand that the extension of the therapy work to nontherapy hours allows for a greater therapeutic focus. Burns and Auerbach (1992) have found that "differences in homework compliance are significantly correlated with recovery from depression" (p. 464). The homework might involve having the client complete an activity schedule (an excellent homework for the first session), complete several DTRs, or try new behaviors. The homework needs to flow from the session material, rather than being tacked onto the end of the session simply because CBT should include homework. The more meaningful and collaborative the homework, the greater the likelihood of client compliance with the therapeutic regimen.

Termination

The goal of CBT is not cure, but more effective coping. As a skill-building model of psychotherapy, the therapist's goal is to assist clients in acquiring the skills to deal with the internal and external stressors. The termination is accomplished gradually, to allow time for ongoing modifications and corrections. Sessions are tapered off from once weekly to biweekly, to a monthly basis, with follow-up sessions at 3 and 6 months, until therapy is ended. Clients can, of course, still call and set an appointment in the event of an emergency.

CONCLUSION

As demonstrated above, there is much in common between AP and CBT. Furthermore, both approaches have much to offer each other. Thus, we believe that cognitive therapists and Adlerian psychotherapists would enrich their theoretical orientation and clinical practice with a deeper understanding of the psychology of Alfred Adler and of CBT, respectively.

REFERENCES

Adler, A. (1937). Significance of early recollections. *International Journal of Individual Psychology, 3,* 283–287.
Adler, A. (1964). Brief comments on reason, intelligence, and feeble-mindedness. In H. L. Ansbacher & R. R. Ansbacher (Eds.), *Superiority and social interest: A collection of later writings* (pp. 41–49). New York: Norton.
Ansbacher, H. L., & Ansbacher, R. R. (Eds.). (1956). *The Individual Psychology of Alfred Adler.* New York: Harper & Row.
Ansbacher, H. L., & Ansbacher, R. R. (Eds.). (1964). *Superiority and social interest: A collection of later writings.* New York: Norton.
Bandura, A. (1977). *Social learning theory.* Englewood Cliffs, NJ: Prentice-Hall.
Beck, A. T. (1991). *Beck scale for suicidal ideation.* San Antonio, TX: Psychological Corporation.

Beck, A. T. (1993a). *Beck anxiety inventory.* San Antonio, TX: Psychological Corporation.
Beck, A. T. (1993b). *Beck hopelessness scale.* San Antonio, TX: Psychological Corporation.
Beck, A. T., Freeman, A., and Associates (1990). *Cognitive therapy of personality disorders.* New York: Guilford.
Beck, A. T., Rush, A. J., Shaw, B. F., & Emery, G. (1979). *Cognitive therapy of depression.* New York: Guilford.
Beck, A. T., Steer, R. A., & Brown, G. K. (1996). *Beck depression inventory-II.* San Antonio, TX: Psychological Corporation.
Burns, D. D., & Auerbach, A. H. (1992). Does homework compliance enhance recovery from depression. *Psychiatric Annals, 22,* 464–469.
Bruhn, A. (1990). *Earliest childhood memories: Vol. 1. Theory and application to clinical practice.* New York: Praeger.
Bruhn, A., & Last, J. (1982). Earliest childhood memories: Four theoretical perspectives. *Journal of Personality Assessment, 46,* 119–127.
Dowd, E., & Kelly, F. (1980). Adlerian psychology and cognitive behavioral therapy: Convergences. *Journal of Individual Psychology, 36,* 119–135.
Ellis, A. (1985). Expanding the ABC's of RET. In M. Mahoney & A. Freeman (Eds.), *Cognition and psychotherapy* (pp. 313–324). New York: Plenum.
Ellis, A. (1989). The history of cognition in psychotherapy. In A. Freeman, K. M. Simon, L. Beutler, & H. Arkowitz (Eds.), *Comprehensive handbook of cognitive therapy* (pp. 5–20). New York: Plenum.
Forgus, R., & Shulman, B. H. (1979). *Personality: A cognitive view.* Englewood Cliffs, NJ: Prentice-Hall.
Freeman, A., & Boyll, S. (1992). The use of dreams and the dream metaphor in cognitive-behavior therapy. *Psychotherapy in Private Practice, 10,* 173–192.
Freeman, A., Simon, K. M., Pretzer, J., & Fleming, B. (1990). *Clinical applications of cognitive therapy.* New York: Plenum
Hall, C., & Lindzey, G. (1970). *Theories of personality* (2nd ed.). New York: John Wiley.
Layden, M. A., Newman, C., Freeman, A., & Morse, S. (1993). *Cognitive therapy of borderline personality disorder.* Boston: Allyn & Bacon.
Lingg, M., & Kottman, T. (1991). Changing mistaken beliefs through visualization of early recollections. *Individual Psychology, 47,* 255–260.
Mahoney, M. J. (1974). *Cognition and behavior modification.* Cambridge, MA: Ballinger.
Manaster, G., & Corsini, R. (1982). *Individual Psychology.* Itasca, IL: Peacock.
Mosak, H. H. (1995). Adlerian psychotherapy. In R. J. Corsini & D. Wedding (Eds.), *Current psychotherapies* (5th ed., pp. 51–94). Itasca, IL: Peacock.
Newman, B., & Newman, P. (1995). *Development through life: A psychosocial approach.* Pacific Grove, CA: Brooks/Cole.
Rosen, H. (1985). *Piagetian concepts of clinical relevance.* New York: Columbia University Press.
Rosen, H. (1989). Piagetian theory and cognitive therapy. In A. Freeman, K. M. Simon, L. Beutler, & H. Arkowitz (Eds.), *Comprehensive handbook of cognitive therapy* (pp. 189–212). New York: Plenum.

Safran, J. D., & Segal, Z. S. (1990). *Interpersonal process in cognitive therapy.* New York: Basic Books.

Shulman, B. H. (1985). Cognitive therapy and the Individual Psychology of Alfred Adler. In M. Mahoney & A. Freeman (Eds.), *Cognition and psychotherapy* (pp. 243–258). New York: Plenum.

Part 3
Cognitive, Adlerian, and Constructivist Responses

6

Adlerian, Cognitive-Behavioral, and Constructivist Psychotherapies: Commonalities, Differences, and Integration

E. Thomas Dowd

Knowledge is unity. Like the fabled blind men examining the elephant, the different theories, conceptualizations, and techniques used to explain and orchestrate psychological and behavioral stasis and change are merely different ways of looking at the same phenomena. Theories of psychopathology and psychotherapy are fundamentally conceptual pegs upon which to hang and direct therapeutic interventions. No mental health practitioner can possibly pay attention to the full range of cognitive, behavioral, or emotional phenomena nor consider the full range of possible interventions. To which phenomena therapists turn their attention, and how, where, and when they intervene, is determined, in large part, by the theory to which they adhere. Which theories, explanatory constructs, and interventions we use depends on several factors.

First, theories and techniques become prominent because of the particular zeitgeist (the spirit of the times). Early psychoanalysis, drawing on nineteenth century physical science, was heavily mechanical and hydraulic in nature, reflecting the scientific culture of its time. The concept of symptom substitution is an example. Later, Carl Rogers's client-centered therapy was introspective and democratic, reflecting the new post-World War II affluence and the spread of democratic ideals. It was also a "reaction formation" from the perceived authoritarianism of psychodynamic approaches. Behavior therapy came of age in the technologically obsessed American culture of the 1960s (remember James Bond's gadgets?), in which it was assumed that technology could solve all our problems. Early cognitive therapy, with its focus on the transmission and storage of cognitive content, reflected the new interest in computer technology. The mind was thought to be a high-level computer, storing memories and other data accurately on its hard drive. It too was a reaction formation from the inability of behavior therapy to accurately predict behavioral output from antecedent events and reinforcing consequences. Significant error variance resided in the "black box." Latter-day cognitive therapy, with its focus on schema-focused therapy, was heavily influenced by the newer understanding of the brain as a constructor of reality, rather than as a storage receptacle. It also was influenced by worldwide travel and communications, which led to the inescapable conclusion that different people in different cultures interpreted events and situations very differently. Different cultures rubbing against each other, as never before in human history, led to a heightened sense of cultural relativism and the construction of reality. I have applied this type of analysis in more detail in tracing the history and development of cognitive psychotherapy (Dowd, 2002a).

Second, theories and techniques become prominent because of the psychology of the founder. Freudian psychoanalysis may have become somewhat rigid in its formulations because its founder had strong convictions about many things. The democratic emphasis of client-centered therapy may have derived in part from Rogers's early training as a minister. Adlerian psychology's (AP's) democratic emphasis probably derived from Alfred Adler's European social democratic political views. I have noted that the constructivist point of view is often held by individuals who appear unusually able to hold ostensibly conflicting views in their minds simultaneously. They also seem to be unusually open to change and to simply enjoy the interplay of ideas for their own sake. Perhaps this is an extension of the oft-noted perception that mental health professionals tend to write and practice in areas of personal meaning for them.

Third, the sociology of professionalism accounts for some theory development. At least in the academic world, professionals become famous and influential because they develop new systems of therapy that they then proclaim represent a tremendous advance over existing systems. Indeed, when these approaches are fresh, they do seem to possess a greater power to cure—perhaps because of the social influence, persuasive power, and charisma of the founder. Second-generation proponents, who often lack the single-minded and passionate devotion to "the cause" possessed by the founder, may have more difficulty obtaining equally impressive results. Hence the "Dodo bird effect" noted by Luborsky, Singer, and Luborsky (1975). In the history of psychotherapy research, it is rare that any system produces better outcomes than any other, and then only in circumscribed situations (Lambert & Bergin, 1994), although Chambless (2001) has noted that this finding is based on research with adult outpatients. However, no professionals have ever become famous by claiming that they do much the same things as others do, but use different names. Hence, as I noted years ago (Dowd, 1981), there has been a tendency for cognitive-behavioral therapy (CBT) to expand conceptually, leading to a real danger that, as it becomes well-known, others will claim that is what they have been doing all along, but have just been calling it by different names. The boundaries of systems of therapies, which initially are firmly drawn, become increasingly fuzzy and overlap with other systems over time (Dowd, 2002a). With the exception of Dollard and Miller, only recently has anyone obtained much professional mileage from *integration*. Now there is an organization (Society for the Exploration of Psychotherapy Integration), whose entire rationale and activity is integration, and several prominent psychologists are strongly affiliated with it, although they attained prominence prior to their affiliation with the integration movement.

Fourth, what theories and interventions we use depend in part on the education we receive and the literature we read. For example, those who matriculated from counseling psychology or counselor education programs may be trained to a greater extent in Rogerian or other humanistic approaches; those who graduated from clinical psychology programs may have learned more about Freudian and behavioral approaches. Some of these and other program differences have lessened in recent years, but others remain. Our graduate education then predisposes us to read certain literatures and attend certain conferences. Clinical psychologists attend conventions of the American Psychological Association and the Association for Advancement of Behavior Therapy, counselor educators attend conventions of the American Counseling Association, and counseling psychologists may attend either or both.

Even within the same theoretical orientation, professionals may not be aware of the ideas of others, if they belong to different disciplines. For example, Aaron Beck and Albert Ellis were long unaware of the contributions by each other, because Beck is a psychiatrist (who read the medical literature) and Ellis is a psychologist (who read the psychological literature). This has been a particular problem for Adlerian psychologists in attempting to disseminate their ideas, because they have their own organization (The North American Society of Adlerian Psychology) and have tended to operate within their own circle, talking primarily to each other. It is difficult for professionals to break out of their established organizations and literature. Several years ago, there was a move to associate (in relatively unspecified ways) the North American Society of Adlerian Psychology with the International Association for Cognitive Psychotherapy, resulting in expressions of consternation, perhaps, on both sides.

Despite these encapsulatory tendencies, however, there have been some attempts to examine the commonalities among CBT, constructivism, and AP. Most of these attempts have been between the first two; indeed, part of the constructivist approach to therapy may be seen as an outgrowth of an expanded view of CBT (Dowd, 2002a). An example of this attempt at integration is the recent book edited by Michael Mahoney (1995). Although it consists mostly of representatives of both camps talking in parallel streams, Mahoney's introductory chapter does provide his own attempt at integration, through an examination of these two approaches in several different dimensions.

Mahoney's first dimension is the distinction between the rationalist and the constructivist philosophies, in which the former stresses the acquisition and storage of information and assumes an invariant reality (which may be incorrectly perceived or interpreted), and the latter stresses the proactive nature of human cognition and the relativity of reality. From my reading of the chapter in this volume, I would place AP squarely in the constructivist camp. For example, Watts and Shulman (this volume) discuss the common origin of Adlerian and constructivist therapies in the philosophical writings of Kant and Vaihinger. The concepts of holism and *lifestyle* (Jones & Lyddon, this volume) are constructivist in nature. When representatives of CBT first became aware of Mahoney's distinction they immediately insisted that CBT also was constructivist. Rationalism quickly became far less meaningful.

Mahoney's second dimension is that of social, biological, and embodiment issues—the increasing acceptance of social and biological factors in psychological disorders. Emotional expression and attachment are also important here. Adlerian psychology was always social in nature; indeed, through the concept of *social interest,* one might argue that is its central construct. Watts and Shulman and Freeman and Urschel (this volume) speak of the social embeddedness of experience. Constructivist therapies, likewise, because of their experiential nature, can also be seen as heavily social. CBT has become more so, with its increasing emphasis on the role of emotional expression, the therapeutic relationship, and schemas.

Mahoney's third dimension is that of the role of unconscious processes. Constructivists give heavy importance to this dimension, through their emphasis on the principle of self-organization and core ordering processes (e.g., Guidano, 1991). Adlerian psychology too appears to accept unconscious processes, although not explicitly by that name (were the originators too close to Freud's time?). Rather, it must be inferred from such concepts as guiding fictions, lifestyle analysis, the realm of meanings, and the teleological principle. CBT began to incorporate some aspects of unconscious processing and knowledge (I prefer the terms *implicit learning* and *tacit knowledge*), with its recent focus on schemas (e.g., Young, 1999). There has also been an increasing attempt to link the experimental psychology literature on tacit knowledge with cognitive therapy (e.g., Dowd, 2002b; Dowd & Courchaine, 1996; Fleming, Heikkinen, & Dowd, 1992; Stein & Young, 1992; Tatryn, Nadel, & Jacobs, 1989). Not all cognitive behavior therapists feel comfortable with this trend, however.

Mahoney's fourth dimension is that of self and systems dynamics—essentially a renewal of the psychology of the self. Adlerian and constructivist approaches appear to have always stressed the basic aspect of *selfhood* as a unifying core cognitive construct. Mahoney himself, as a constructivist, has repeatedly used this term (e.g., Mahoney, 1991). Adler's *schema of apperception* (Sperry, this volume), as well as *lifestyle,* would seem to fall into this category. So, for that matter, does the concept of *resistance,* what Adlerians call "neurotic safeguarding" (Sperry, this volume) or "compensation" (Watts & Shulman, this volume). The concept has entered the CBT literature in a much less comprehensive fashion, although Mahoney (1991) has written on the self-protective nature of resistance, and Dowd (1999, 2001) has written about the place of its close cousin, psychological reactance, in the psychopathology and the therapeutic process.

Mahoney's fifth dimension is emotionality and experiential emphasis. Constructivism has always been highly experiential and has relied on emotional expression as a curative factor. It was difficult, however, for me to decide, from these chapters, the place of emotionality and experience in AP. Like first-generation CBT, it appears to be a highly analytical, cognitive approach. However, conducting any form of psychotherapy without some consideration of emotional phenomena is very difficult, so perhaps it is there in tacit form. As mentioned above, CBT has recently begun to pay more explicit attention to the role of emotional processing.

Mahoney's sixth dimension is the role of both constructivism and CBT in the integration movement. Mahoney's (1995) book itself can be seen as an attempt at the integration of these two systems. Each system has profoundly influenced the other, and the recent conceptual expansion of Beck's cognitive therapy has led some writers to suggest that CBT itself is an integrative theory (Alford & Norcross, 1991; Dowd, 2002a). Indeed, several authors primarily identified with CBT (including myself) also publish in the *Journal of Psychotherapy Integration* and have an affiliation with the integration movement. Constructivism also brings to CBT an emphasis on developmental processes, the creation of self-knowledge, and the entire literature on attachment theory (e.g., Bowlby, 1988). CBT brings to constructivism a considerable technology of interventions, based on research, as well as a comprehensive theory of the cognitive aspects of personality and psychopathology.

This volume represents one of the few attempts to bring AP into the integration movement and, as such, is very welcome. However, Adlerian psychologists appear to have been aware of integration before. For example, Allen (1978) complained that the behavior therapy of that time, in "going cognitive," had returned implicitly to earlier formulations of the therapeutic change process. Adler, he suggested, had said it all earlier.

One of the first attempts to integrate AP and CBT was made by Dowd and Kelly (1980) and was published in the *Journal of Individual Psychology*. They wrote at a time when CBT was just being developed from behavior therapy and well before the later focus on personality disorders, developmental aspects of psychopathology, and the constructivist infiltration. They identified a number of dimensions along which to compare the two systems. With the emerging cognitive emphasis in behavior therapy at that time, CBT was beginning to approach the strong cognitive emphasis in AP—a trend that has continued. Both systems were primarily ideographic in nature, although AP was much more interested in the social context of human action than CBT, which was mostly intrapsychic.

In general, mainstream CBT retains this intrapsychic focus, although perhaps with a somewhat greater appreciation for the social context of behavior. Adlerian psychology is mostly holistic and synthesizing in orientation; at that time, CBT was still mostly reductionistic and analytical in nature. With the increasing emphasis on core cognitive themes and schemas fostered by cognitive therapy of personality disorders (Beck, Freeman, & Associates, 1990; Young, 1999), present-day CBT has become more similar to the thematic and holistic nature of AP.

In two areas identified by Dowd and Kelly (1980), however, AP and CBT diverge even today, although the differences are probably less pronounced. Adlerian psychology is a subjective, phenomenological approach, which might be described as long on theory and short on data. By contrast, CBT has long stressed the primacy of observable, objective data and the necessity for phenomena to be observable to external agents, to be of scientific interest and psychologically valid. This is a central reason why CBT has been in the forefront of the empirically supported treatments movement. On the other hand, it historically left behavioral therapy with a rather impoverished theoretical base, which has been partially rectified by the more elaborate conceptual infrastructure of CBT. Constructivist approaches further added to this conceptual elaboration, although much of its research base is located in the experimental psychology literature and attachment theory. Indeed, if future integration is warranted, it is likely to be integration between the literatures in various aspects of experimental psychology and psychotherapy, rather than among different systems of psychotherapy, as in the past.

The last dimension of comparison made by Dowd and Kelly (1980) was that involving the locus of behavioral motivation and probably will remain a point of difference. Adlerian psychology has long emphasized that behavior is purposive and goal-directed—in other words, future-oriented—referred to as the *teleological principle*. These goals are seen as the organizing and controlling factors behind all behavior, so that behavior is governed by the anticipation or expectation of future events. What is not apparent, at least to me, is how explicit these goals are. If they are relatively implicit in nature, they begin to approach conceptually the CBT idea of core cognitive schemas or tacit knowledge structures (Dowd & Courchaine, 1996). Conversely, behavioral theory in 1980 was based on the idea, supported by considerable research, that behavior is governed by its consequences; in other words, what occurred in the past, by way of differential reinforcement. Antecedent stimuli (e.g., goals, expectancies), although they might function as cuing stimuli to trigger behavior, cannot reinforce (and therefore motivate) it. In cognitive-behavioral theory, core or tacit knowledge is likewise not seen as possessing motivational or reinforcement power, although it might channel and direct behavior. Thus, CBT, by extension, is based on the assumption that the motivating source of behavior lies in past consequences, rather than in future goals, and that these motivating reinforcers arise from external sources, rather than from intrapsychic events.

The only way in which future-oriented goals or expectancies might act as reinforcers is discussed by Bandura (1977). He stated that the representation of future consequences may be an important source of motivation as people establish performance goals, then make self-rewarding reactions contingent upon the achievement of these performance goals. Furthermore, because of the symbolic ability of humans, it may be that the perception of reinforcement is more powerful than actual reinforcement. However, this future expectancy is ultimately based on a past external reinforcement history of a relatively consistent nature. Goals do not arise within a reinforcement vacuum.

Let me examine one more Adlerian-like idea. The teleological principle states that behavior is future-oriented toward a goal. By contrast, the *teleonomic principle* (Mahoney, 1982) refers to "inherent ordering processes which serve to direct the maintenance and growth of open systems" (p. 112). In other words, teleology refers to purposive behavior toward an explicit or implicit goal; teleonomy refers to purposive movement without a specific goal, but in the service of organismic growth and creativity. But, what is the reinforcer in teleonomy? Is teleonomy really creative organismic growth over time, or is it (as a behaviorist might say) directed and channeled by tacit reinforcers (in other words, is it really consequential, rather than purposive)? Like Harry Harlow's monkeys, do we obtain reinforcement from added stimulation itself? Are we motivated by motivation? Is there an optimal level of stimulation to which humans aspire? If so, are there individual differences in this desired level? Can this level change over time? "These are deep waters, Watson!"

Let me carry the teleonomic implications one step further, and apply them to comparison and contrast among AP, CBT, and constructivism. The three laws of thermodynamics reside on the border of physics and chemistry, in physical chemistry. The first law is about the conservation of matter and energy and states that the sum total in the universe is a constant: Its most famous explication is the $E = MC^2$ equation. The second law is also known as the "law of entropy" (Mahoney, 1991) and states that, in any spontaneous process, the disorder in the universe is increasing toward an ultimately random distribution of matter and energy. The higher the level of entropy, the higher the level of disorder; thus the universe is gradually moving toward disorder (running down, if you will). Furthermore, more order in one place means less order in another. The third law states that all molecular motion ceases at absolute zero (−450°C).

The picture of the universe, and by implication everything in it (including humans), postulated by the first and second laws, is depressing. A wag once said that the first law says you can't win, and the second law says you can't break even. Such a picture, however, seemed at variance with emerging data in biology and other life sciences (Mahoney, 1991). However, the chemist Ilya Prigogine (1980) demonstrated that the second law of thermodynamics applied only to closed (thermodynamically isolated) systems, in which neither matter nor energy could enter or depart. Closed systems aim toward homeostasis or a steady state, much as early behavior therapy implicitly assumed. The law of entropy, Prigogine showed, does not apply to open systems in which both matter and energy can be exchanged with its environment; in these systems, new structures of increasing order and complexity can spontaneously arise from the interaction effects of the perturbations stemming from internal processes and ongoing engagements with the environment. Open systems (of which humans are an example) exist as an uneasy balance of equilibrium and disequilibrium. Thus, order can truly emerge out of chaos as open system organisms strive to create structures of greater complexity and differentiation: a phenomenon of chaos theory. The parallel with the assimilation and accommodation opponent processes, postulated by Jean Piaget, is striking.

The principles of chaos theory (or nonlinear dynamics) as an example of teleonomy can be applied to self-awareness and the psychotherapy process. For example, Amunategui and Dowd (1998) used nonlinear modeling procedures to examine the relationship between cardiac autonomic dynamics and the self-relevance of contextual stimuli. They found a significantly greater degree of complexity in plot topography related to cardiac activity dynamics with increasingly self-relevant stimulus content.

How does this relate to AP, CBT, and constructivism? Applications of chaos theory and principles of self-organizing systems to psychotherapy are based on and follow logically from constructivism, which is heavily teleonomic in nature. Furthermore, insofar as AP suggests an active and evolutionary process in which perceptions and cognitions are applied to new functions, while new cognitive structures are developed to serve old functions in new situations (Freeman & Urschel, this volume), it postulates a similar self-organizing cognitive process. However, because of its reliance on teleology rather than teleonomy, AP may be less purely constructivist. The structural differentiation model, implicit in the open systems approach to human behavior, seems to be present in constructivism, and, to a lesser extent, in AP and is powerfully optimistic in its assumption of the possibility of significant human change. It postulates that individuals constantly undergo change as their cognitive-structural assumptions interact—and often clash—with their environment, in a constant oscillative process. Psychotherapy is simply one mechanism for the potential creation of significant change. Religion and spirituality, similar to psychotherapy in their profound meaning-changing potentials, are others (Dowd, 1997).

CBT, by contrast, began from a different epistemology. It shares with AP and constructivism an optimistic assumption about the possibility of human change, but this change is based on changing reinforcement contingencies for behavior, not cognitive structures. Early cognitive therapy (e.g., Beck, Rush, Shaw, & Emery, 1979) was devoted to changing the cognitive content and distortions behind emotional problems, not the structures underlying them. However, with the advent of cognitive therapy for personality disorders (Beck, Freeman & Associates, 1990; Young, 1999), CBT began to approach AP and constructivism in its appreciation for and consideration of change in self-organizing cognitive systems (i.e., schemas). Along with this tripartite rapprochement, however, has come a new appreciation of the difficulty of fostering truly significant cognitive, emotional, and behavioral change that persists (Chambless, 2001), a phenomenon predicted earlier by Mahoney (1982, 1991) in discussing the tremendous (and appropriate) resistance to change by the human cognitive system. This is at variance with the optimistic implications, especially, of the constructivist movement. Truly, it appears, the more we change, the more we remain the same!

Now, let me provide a more specific examination and analysis of the chapters contained in this volume. They are all excellent and form as comprehensive an exploration of the similarities and differences among the three systems as we are likely to receive for some time. There is significant overlap among them, as would be expected, given the tacit similarities of many of the constructs in each system.

The two chapters by Sperry and by Freeman and Urschel (this volume) include many of the same themes from different perspectives.

Both AP and CBT are collaborative in nature, involve both cognitions and behaviors, follow an educational model, and help the client to develop alternative cognitive and behavioral skills. Both were created partly as reactions to the excesses and overelaboration of metaphorical constructs in culture-bound Freudian thought. In addition, more recent CBT emphases on schema identification and change, the importance of meaning structures in human functioning, and continuous cognitive development throughout the life span have aligned it more closely with AP's concept of the lifestyle and the importance of early recollections. Furthermore, the new emphasis on the dynamics of resistance and stasis in CBT closely parallels the compensation strategy of Adler; in both systems, resistance is seen as healthy and adaptive, rather than pathological—as something to be worked with rather than against. Unclear to me, however, is how systematic desensitization fits into the Adlerian system, as discussed by Sperry.

The two chapters by Watts and Shulman and by Jones and Lyddon (this volume), on the similarities and differences between AP and constructivism, illustrate, even more dramatically, the close relationship of these two approaches; indeed, the two seem to be similar variations on the same theme. My reading of AP, as an outsider, is that it was, from its inception, heavily constructive in nature, although not in title. The tracing of its philosophical lineage to Kant and Vaihinger further reinforces this view.

Missing, for the sake of conceptual elegance and completeness, is a comparison of CBT and constructivism. However, that has been provided by Mahoney (1995), and I have discussed some comparisons earlier. In any event, CBT is now heavily imbued with constructivist overtones, so the similarities might outweigh the differences.

Adlerian psychology and CBT each have much to offer the other, as these chapters point out. In addition to its emphasis on the collaborative relationship, CBT has developed an impressive armamentarium of specific change-inducing methods (McMullin, 1986), augmented by such Adlerian-derived techniques as paradoxical interventions (Dowd & Trutt, 1988). Adlerian psychology, by contrast, has tended to be more global and idiosyncratic in its approach to therapy. CBT, on the other hand, has historically lacked the rich theoretical underpinning that has characterized AP, but, in recent years, that has changed considerably. However, much of CBT's expanded theoretical base has been borrowed from other systems (e.g., attachment theory, constructivism). Perhaps this difference reflects their different origins: AP's in post-Freudian theorizing and CBTs in American empirical psychology. In addition, AP has always included a social dimension to human activity that CBT has only recently begun to consider. Finally, the notion of secondary gain has played a more prominent role in AP than in CBT.

Other differences may be more difficult to reconcile. As I discussed earlier, CBT, like behavior therapy before it, is fundamentally based on a reinforcement model; past events and their reinforcers (or lack thereof) shape human behavior in profound ways. Adlerian psychology, by contrast, has stressed the goal-directed and purposive nature of human activity. In other words, CBT is consequential in nature, and AP is anticipatory. Arguing which is true is likely to be as unproductive as the old nature versus nurture controversy that has oscillated throughout psychology's brief existence and continues to plague us to this day.

Although not satisfying to zealots on either side, it is likely that both consequences and anticipations shape human behavior in a reciprocal fashion. Even accepting this, however, professionals can still (and probably will) disagree about which is primal (i.e., the first cause). I would still argue that, fundamentally, human behavior and cognition are shaped by reinforcing consequences specific to each culture and that teleonomic and teleological activity is a later development that is dependent upon the values of that culture, as well as upon the cultural reinforcement of certain activities. It is likely that purposive behavior operates only within limits set by the reinforcing contingencies of the individual's culture and by his or her own biological and genetic characteristics. As Luria (1976) has discussed, even fundamental cognitive activities, such as concept formation and interpersonal awareness, are determined by cultural and social variables.

In addition, there is evidence that behavioral activity precedes and shapes cognition, rather than the reverse (Hobbs, 1962; Schachter & Singer, 1962). This is difficult for us to observe, because all of us are embedded within the values and assumptions (a form of tacit knowledge) of our own culture and cannot easily escape from them nor examine them from an outside perspective. Ironically, constructivism itself would probably support this position. In addition, like Adlerian psychologists, I see social and family activity as the primary venues for these culturally shaped processes to occur.

The theoretical richness of AP has both strengths and weaknesses. On one hand, it provides direction for practitioners and explanations for why interventions do and do not work. On the other hand, some of the concepts (like many of Freud's) now appear dated, culture-specific, and epiphenomenal, contributing perhaps to the perception that AP is relatively encapsulated and theoretically inert. But the behavioral and cognitive therapies, however much they have changed and grown over the years, can easily appear as a collection of techniques in search of a theory, held together primarily by pragmatism and technical eclecticism. Constructivism, because of its amorphous nature, runs an even greater risk in this regard. For example, although possessing a set of assumptions, CBT has only occasionally (e.g., Dowd, 2002b; Dowd & Courchaine, 1996; Fleming et al., 1992; Stein & Young, 1992; Tatryn et al., 1989) drawn on the comprehensive and rich theoretical explanations available in cognitive science or experimental psychology.

Human cognitive activity is a complex and mysterious phenomenon. Much of what we call cognition appears to lie beyond conscious awareness (Kihlstrom, 1987) and therefore may appear counterintuitive. There is evidence, drawn from the experimental psychology literature (see Dowd & Courchaine, 1996; Reber, 1993), indicating that tacit knowledge (the "unconscious," if you will) holds evolutionary primacy, is more influential than explicit knowledge, and is less amenable to change. Memory itself appears to be divided and at least as constructed as it is stored (Dowd, 2002b; Dowd & Courchaine, 1996; Fleming et al., 1992). Tacit cognitive rules and assumptions, which form the basis of our "personal-cognitive organization" (Guidano, 1991), are fundamental to our sense of personal identity and integrity and are not easily changed. Cognitive structures, once laid down, are very resistant to incorporating discrepant external data (Dowd & Seibel, 1990) and thus tend to perpetuate themselves. New events tend to be interpreted according to the cognitive rules we already possess, known as "self-perpetuating algorithms" (Lewicki, Hill, & Czyzewska, 1992), so that we see what we expect to see and find what we expect to find. Early events are powerful determinants of later tacit assumptions and guide later implicit and explicit learning. These assumptions act like cognitive filters, to ensure that subsequent events are interpreted in ways consistent with our existing cognitive schemas. We all tend to find that for which we are looking, and that tendency is probably responsible for the creation of various systems of psychotherapy in the first place.

In the end, however, one might ask if any of this makes a difference. Brand-name psychotherapies, like brand-name religions, are of increasingly less interest to increasingly more professionals. Over one half of current practitioners now describe themselves as cognitive-behavioral in orientation, but it is difficult to know to what extent this reflects a real allegiance and practice, based on a detailed knowledge of its theory and interventions, or simply a realization that CBT is the major empirically supported therapy and that they had better get on board if they wish their practice to be reimbursable. Adlerian psychology has not been an option to officially consider, and constructivism is probably too vague and interventionally diffuse to be a contender. I am less interested in what psychotherapists call themselves than in what they do and how successful they are, just as I am less interested in which religion someone claims membership than in what they believe and (even more importantly) practice.

Finally, all of us should be cognizant of the research findings on the effects of psychotherapy of any kind. According to Chambless (2001), at least one third of clients do not benefit from our interventions. In addition, the relapse rate is high. In reviewing the effects of approximately 1,100 studies, Orlinsky and Howard (1986) summarized the question of what is responsible for effective therapy, as follows:

> Our provisional answer to the question is as follows: (1) The patient's and the therapist's therapeutic bond—that is their reciprocal role investment, empathic resonance and mutual affirmation—is effectively therapeutic, (2) Certain therapeutic interventions, when done skillfully with suitable patients, are effectively therapeutic, (3) Patients and therapists focusing their interventions on the patient's feelings is effectively therapeutic, (4) Preparing the patient adequately for participation in therapy and collaborative sharing of responsibility for problem solving are effectively therapeutic, (5) Within certain limits more rather than less therapy is effectively therapeutic. (p. 371)

Blocher (2000) comments on this summary as follows:

> Essentially 1,100 studies yielded a set of conclusions that are likely to be known intuitively by any graduate student who has successfully completed one semester of practicum: The relationship is important; some things work with some clients better than others; try to stay with the client's feelings; structure with the client what counseling is all about, and be sure the client knows his or her responsibility for what happens; counseling works better if you can keep the client going past the third interview. (p. 274)

Blocher goes on to say that the results reviewed in the fourth edition of the *Handbook of Psychotherapy and Behavior Change* were not greatly different. These results should give pause to all of us, whatever our theoretical orientation.

The stuff of which therapies of all brands is made does not differ greatly from that which comprises effective human relations of all kinds.

People and institutions (such as religions) had been helping (as well as hurting) other people for centuries before the "talking cure" and its derivatives were invented. Many of the therapies that were subsequently developed seemed designed more to advance the careers of the developers than to assist hurting people. Therefore, I applaud this excellent attempt to integrate AP, CBT, and constructivism.

REFERENCES

Alford, B. A., & Norcross, J. C. (1991). Cognitive therapy as integrative therapy. *Journal of Psychotherapy Integration, 1,* 175–190.
Allen, T. W. (1978). On the reinvention of the wheel, the franchising of science, and other pastimes. *The Counseling Psychologist, 7,* 37–42.
Amunategui, L. F., & Dowd, E. T. (1998, July). Nonlinear analyses of time series data sets with personal computer platforms. Presentation at the World Congress of Behaviour and Cognitive Therapies, Acapulco, Mexico.
Bandura, A. (1977). Self-efficacy: Toward a unifying theory of behavior change. *Psychological Review, 84,* 191–215.
Beck, A. T., Freeman, A., & Associates (1990). *Cognitive therapy of personality disorders.* New York: Guilford.
Beck, A. T., Rush, A. J., Shaw, B. F., & Emery, G. (1979). *Cognitive therapy of depression.* New York: Guilford.
Blocher, D. H. (2000). *The evolution of counseling psychology.* New York: Springer.
Bowlby, J. (1988). *A secure base.* New York: Basic Books.
Chambless, D. L. (2001, November). Invited address. Association for Advancement of Behavior Therapy, Philadelphia.
Dowd, E. T. (1981). Cognitive behavior therapy: Dangers and new directions. *Academic Psychology Bulletin, 3,* 387–394.
Dowd, E. T. (1997, September). What makes people really change? And why is it so difficult? Symposium presentation at the 27th Congress of the European Association for Behaviour and Cognitive Therapies, Venice, Italy.
Dowd, E. T. (1999). Toward a briefer therapy: Overcoming resistance and reactance in the therapeutic process. In W. J. Matthews & J. H. Edgette (Eds.), *Current thinking and research in brief therapy* (Vol. 3, pp. 263–286). Philadelphia: Brunner/Mazel.
Dowd, E. T. (2001). Developmental correlates of psychological reactance. *Journal of Cognitive Psychotherapy: An International Quarterly, 15,* 239–272.
Dowd, E. T. (2002a). History and recent developments in cognitive psychotherapy. In R. L. Leahy & E. T. Dowd (Eds.), *Clinical advances in cognitive psychotherapy* (pp. 15–28). New York: Springer.
Dowd, E. T. (2002b). Memory processes in psychotherapy: Implications for integration. *Journal of Psychotherapy Integration, 12,* 233–246.
Dowd, E. T., & Courchaine, K. E. (1996). Implicit learning, tacit knowledge, and implications for stasis and change in cognitive psychotherapy. *Journal of Cognitive Psychotherapy: An International Quarterly, 10,* 163–180.

Dowd, E. T., & Kelly, F. D. (1980). Adlerian psychology and cognitive-behavior therapy: Convergences. *Journal of Individual Psychology, 36,* 119–135.

Dowd, E. T., & Seibel, C. A. (1990). A cognitive theory of resistance and reactance: Implications for treatment. *Journal of Mental Health Counseling, 12,* 458–469.

Dowd, E. T., & Trutt, S. D. (1988). Paradoxical interventions in behavior modification. In M. Hersen, R. M. Eisler, & P. M. Miller (Eds.), *Progress in behavior modification, Vol. 23* (pp. 96–130). Newbury Park, CA: Sage.

Fleming, K., Heikkinen, R., & Dowd, E. T. (1992). Cognitive therapy: The repair of memory. *Journal of Cognitive Psychotherapy: An International Quarterly, 6,* 155–174.

Guidano, V. F. (1991). *The self in process: Towards a post-rationalist cognitive therapy.* New York: Guilford.

Hobbs, N. (1962). Sources of gain in psychotherapy. *American Psychologist, 17,* 741–747.

Kihlstrom, J. F. (1987). The cognitive unconscious. *Science, 237,* 1445–1452.

Lambert, M. J., & Bergin, A. E. (1974). The effectiveness of psychotherapy. In A. E. Bergin & S. L. Garfield (Eds.), *Handbook of psychotherapy and behavior change* (4th ed., pp. 143–189). New York: Wiley.

Lewicki, P., Hill, T., & Czyzewska, M. (1992). Nonconscious acquisition of information. *American Psychologist, 47,* 796–801.

Luborsky, L., Singer, B., & Luborsky, L. (1975). Comparative studies of psychotherapy. *Archives of General Psychiatry, 32,* 995–1008.

Luria, A. R. (1976). *Cognitive development: Its cultural and social foundations.* Cambridge, MA: Harvard University Press.

Mahoney, M. J. (1982). Psychotherapy and the human change process. In J. H. Harvey & M. M. Parks (Eds.), *The Master Lecture Series: Vol. 1. Psychotherapy research and behavior change* (pp. 73–122). Washington, DC: American Psychological Association.

Mahoney, M. J. (1991). *Human change processes.* New York: Basic Books.

Mahoney, M. J. (1995). *Cognitive and constructive psychotherapies: Theory, research, and practice.* New York: Springer.

McMullin, R. (1986). *Handbook of cognitive therapy techniques.* New York: Norton.

Orlinsky, D. E., & Howard, K. I. (1986). Process and outcome in psychotherapy. In S. L. Garfield & A. E. Bergin (Eds.), *Handbook of psychotherapy and behavior change* (3rd ed., pp. 311–384). New York: Wiley.

Prigogine, I. (1980). *From being to becoming: Time and complexity in the physical sciences.* San Francisco: W. H. Freeman.

Reber, A. S. (1993). *Implicit learning and tacit knowledge: An essay on the cognitive unconscious.* New York: Oxford University Press.

Schachter, S., & Singer, J. E. (1962). Cognitive, social, and physiological determinants of emotional state. *Psychological Review, 69,* 379–399.

Stein, D. J., & Young, J. E. (1992). *Cognitive science and clinical disorders.* San Diego: Academic Press.

Tataryn, D. L., Nadel, L., & Jacobs, W. J. (1989). Cognitive therapy and cognitive science. In A. Freeman, K. M. Simon, L. E. Beutler, & H. Arkowitz (Eds.), *Comprehensive handbook of cognitive therapy* (pp. 83–98). New York: Plenum.

Young, J. E. (1999). *Cognitive therapy for personality disorders: A schema-focused approach* (3rd ed.). Sarasota, FL: Professional Resource Press.

7
A Cognitive Conundrum: Where's the Thinking in Cognitive?

Michael P. Maniacci

> So it happens at times that a person believes that he has a world-view, but that there is yet one particular phenomenon that is of such a nature that it baffles the understanding, and that he explains differently and attempts to ignore in order not to harbor the thought that this phenomenon might overthrow the whole view, or that his reflection does not possess enough courage or resolution to penetrate the phenomenon with his world-view.
>
> —Soren Kierkegaard, 1844

> Everything that enters consciousness as "unity" is already tremendously complex: we always have only a semblance of unity.
>
> The phenomenon of the body is the richer, clearer, more tangible phenomenon: to be discussed first, methodologically, without coming to any decision about its ultimate significance.
>
> —Friedrich Nietzsche, 1886–1887

These words, written by Kierkegaard (1844/1980, p. 188), and Nietzsche (1901/1967, p. 270), over 100 years ago, are as relevant today as they were then; Kierkegaard's words are strikingly similar to Adlerian and cognitive theoretical formulations. As the chapters by Watts and Shulman, Jones and Lyddon, Sperry, and Freeman and Urschel have shown, there are many points of convergence between cognitive and constructivist therapies and Adlerian psychology. These authors have done a fine job detailing the similarities and differences between the two perspectives. This chapter briefly highlights what I found most helpful and points the way to six areas both perspectives need to keep in mind if they are going to continue to grow into this new century.

First, this kind of dialogue needs to continue among many schools of psychotherapy. There are far too many systems of psychotherapy articulating many similar constructs. It is almost as if, within each school, the wheel must continually be reinvented. If the dialogue continues, we could save a lot of time. Second, each school has areas that the others may be able to improve. For example, as has been mentioned, the cognitive therapists could benefit from the Adlerian emphasis upon lifestyle assessment techniques for case formulations, and they could also benefit from the Adlerian views on child guidance, counseling, and therapy. The Adlerians could clearly benefit from the cognitive theorists' use of precise language and the constructionists' use of current research from the cognitive sciences and neurosciences.

The authors have done a better job stating their views than I can in such a short chapter. I applaud their work and would like to see even more of it. Yet there is one main area that both Adlerians and cognitive therapies should examine, and that is the area of philosophical underpinnings. The Adlerians have tended to be more philosophically minded than the cognitive-behaviorists and some constructionists (Mosak & Maniacci, 1999), but all could use a somewhat closer examination of the research coming from the cognitive neurosciences. In particular, as mentioned above, there are six main areas that should be more closely scrutinized and are addressed in more detail below.

The philosophical school that has contributed most to this kind of theorizing is phenomenology. Several writers, some of them existential in their philosophical orientation, have done groundbreaking work, not only in their theorizing, but also in their reinterpretation of the research coming from psychologists and neuroscientists on brain–behavior relationships. To name but a few of the leading theorists: Edmund Husserl (1913/1962, 1937/1970), Martin Heidegger (1927/1962, 1954/1968), Jean-Paul Sartre (1943/1956, 1936/1957), Maurice Merleau-Ponty (1946/1962, 1942/1963), and Don Ihde (1977, 1993). My comments are a direct outgrowth of their works; their works were written (in part) in reaction to Hans Vaihinger's intellectual progenitor, Immanuel Kant, an eighteenth century philosopher who had a profound but often unacknowledged influence upon psychology (Hergenhahn, 1997). Vaihinger had a significant influence not only upon Adler (1911/2002, 1956), but upon constructionists also. By expanding upon Kant's work, he brought some helpful concepts into psychology; however, he also brought some conceptual errors, which psychology stills clings to with fervor, but which philosophers have tried to explicate and correct (Husserl, 1937/1970). But more of this later. In this section, I highlight some of the areas that, in my opinion, mark a real growth in the development of psychological theorizing. Both Adlerians and constructionists in particular emphasize these points.

1. Humans are conceptualized as active agents. For decades, humans were thought of as passive receivers of stimulation from their internal or external environments (Gopnik, Meltzoff, & Kuhl, 1999). Of the early theorists who challenged such a notion, two were already mentioned, Alfred Adler and Edmund Husserl; a third was Jean Piaget (1964/1967). All three conceptualized individuals as not simply responding to, but actively shaping, their perceptions and worlds.
2. Humans are conceptualized both from a dynamic and a structural view. When theorists discuss cognitions, schemas, or convictions, they are using the language of structure. When they speak of drives, striving, or desires, they are using the language of dynamics. Both are important, yet many psychologists tend to emphasize one at the expense of the other. The concept of structure provides the "how" and "what" of personality organization. Dynamics provide the "why" it is organized that way and why it resists changing. For example, a client has a belief (i.e., a structure) that declares, "In order to belong, I should please people." The client clings to that belief because it is the way he or she finds his or her place (i.e., striving for significance as a dynamic motivation). Both structure and dynamics are more readily being incorporated into theories in a scientifically sound manner.
3. Humans are conceptualized as having aspects that are both known and unknown. Whether it be labeled conscious and unconscious, common sense and private intelligence, active and dormant schemas, or tacit and implicit knowledge structures, both aspects of personality functioning are being seriously studied in psychology and the cognitive neurosciences (Joseph, 1992). To not take both into account is to deny experience. We do things we do not understand. To acknowledge that is the first step in comprehending why and how we do it.

4. Research from developmental psychology is being integrated into personality theory. For a personality theory to be sound, it must explain not only the existing personality but the developing personality as well (Gopnik et al., 1999). With their emphasis upon how children acquire knowledge structures, constructionists in particular can show a consistency to personality across the life span. Unlike early psychoanalytic constructs, direct experimental work with children is being done and incorporated into personality theory. Using Sartre's (1943/1956) insightful point, humans do not shift ontologically from one type of being as a child to another as an adult: The same philosophical principles that govern the understanding of the human child must apply to understanding the human adult; otherwise, there is a logical inconsistency. For example, humans cannot be conceptualized from a dualistic perspective as adults and from a holistic perspective as children. Philosophically, such a change is the sign of a weak theory, not a scientific observation. Such a shift from one ontological assumption to another is tantamount to changing theories in midstream.

5. The importance of learning and perception is being increasingly explored. In order to understand personality, theorists are increasingly focused upon learning and perception in a more sophisticated, systematic manner. Old notions of stimulus–response and information processing are being replaced by motor theories of the mind, which emphasize feedforward as well as feedback mechanisms. Imprinting, although a part of learning, is no longer considered the cornerstone of such processes.

All these points are encouraging, but there are still some very fuzzy notions about human psychology hanging around our theories. These notions have existed since the ancient Greeks and have been debated in philosophical literature for centuries. Many psychologists, with the notable exception of van Kaam (1969), do not often read philosophy, which is a shame. The philosophers I mentioned above, Husserl, Heidegger, Sartre, Merleau-Ponty, and Ihde, have read psychology in depth and have attempted to address some of the unrecognized paradoxes we have put ourselves into. What they have attempted to demonstrate, both logically and in some cases empirically, is fascinating.

Some of the philosophers have voluntarily been subjects in psychological experiments; others have been welcomed into laboratories to assist

A Cognitive Conundrum: Where's the Thinking in Cognitive?

in research; and still others have actually studied with psychologists for extended periods of time and reinterpreted their research. In most instances, these philosophers have not questioned the utility of the research or writings; they have simply challenged the assumptions behind the conclusions. For example, Merleau-Ponty (1960/1964) was engaged in lecturing about infant and child research for a period of time (and, after his early and untimely death, he was replaced by none other than Jean Piaget). One of the topics he addressed was a child's acquisition of the past tense in language development. He cited as an example a child who was jealous about the birth of his new brother:

> The jealousy that invades the subject when he confirms the arrival of a new brother is essentially a refusal to change his situation. The newcomer is an intruder and is going to confiscate to his own advantage the place in the family that was held until now by our jealous subject. It is in the phase of the "surpassing" of jealousy that one notices the appearance of a link between the affective phenomenon and the linguistic phenomenon: jealousy is overcome thanks to the constitution of a scheme of past-present-future. In effect, jealousy in this subject consists in a rigid attachment to his present—that is, to the situation of the "latest born" which was hitherto his own. . . . For the subject the situation of jealousy is the occasion both for restructuring his relations with the others he lives with and at the same time for acquiring new dimensions of existence (past, present, and future) with the supple play among them. (p. 110)

As Merleau-Ponty demonstrates, acquisition of the linguistic past tense in this child was linked to the social experience of being dethroned (Adler, 1956). Merleau-Ponty's work was not trying to deny the existence of the structural changes in schemas that occur with the acquisition of linguistic learning; he was trying to be holistic, interpersonal, and teleological in interpreting the data, thus adding a dynamic dimension.

The more we speculate about the mind, the more we are confronted with the brain. As Zachar (2000) has documented, psychology is under attack, not only from philosophy, but from neuroscience, biology, and physiologically oriented researchers. What psychologists think is happening in the mind is being put to the test in ways that increasingly are showing the "holes" in our concepts. If psychology is to keep up and not lose any semblance of scientific status, it must begin to pay attention to the holes that it blindly accepts as laws or assumptions. Allow me to elaborate.

Psychologists continue to use the concept of perception. As Husserl (1913/1962) attempted to demonstrate time and again, psychology's understanding of the psychology of perception was in reality an understanding of the physiology of perception. Physiology was considered the basis upon which psychology must be built. Husserl believed that no one yet had adequately explained the psychology of perception, which in itself is different than the physiology of perception. Similarly, Grigsby and Stevens (2000) put it this way:

> It seems probable and useful that psychological theories may be linked to biological theories, and biological theories can be understood in terms of chemical concepts, and chemistry may be explained in terms of physics. Each level of analysis is itself valid, and study of each level may yield significant and important data. Yet it is essential to develop psychological theories which themselves may be understood in terms of more fundamental theories. (p. 14)

While Grigsby and Stevens discuss levels, many in the professional literature are discussing foundations. It is one thing to assume different levels, and quite another to say one level is foundational to the next. If that were the case, psychology would simply be a weak version of biology (or physiology, to be exact). Yet, at the turn of the last century, that was exactly what was happening. Physiology was becoming the foundation for all psychology, and Husserl rejected such a notion. As Zachar (2000) details, that is happening yet again, in no small part because of psychology's well-intentioned but nonetheless overly simplistic views of the human psyche. One such overly simplistic notion he calls the "confabulation problem" (p. 5). He cites studies that show that we do not have "conscious access to many of our higher order cognitive processes" (p. 14), and

> that we distort our present and past attitudes, and that confidence in a memory is unrelated to the accuracy of a memory. Since we often either lack the relevant information or have false information about our cognitive processes, our causal inferences are vulnerable to being chronically inaccurate. These facts are not going to go away. Burying one's head in the sand while waiting for relevant research support is only a temporary solution. (p. 14)

This is hauntingly similar to an insight Nietzsche (1901/1967) originally made in 1888:

> We lack any sensitive organs for this inner world, so we sense a thousandfold complexity as a unity; so we introduce causation where any reason for motion and change remains invisible to us—the sequence of thoughts and feelings is only their becoming visible in consciousness. That this sequence has any-

thing to do with a causal chain is completely unbelievable: consciousness has never furnished us with an example of cause and effect. (pp. 283–284)

For psychology to be up to the challenge, it must clarify its conceptual foundations. This is what Husserl (1913/1962) attempted to do by developing in a systematic manner the principles of phenomenology. He felt that, by systematically studying the structures of consciousness, we would be in a better position to ground all human sciences (e.g., psychology, sociology, and even history) and some of the natural sciences (especially, but not limited to, descriptions of the physical world via technology through perception). The grounding had to be in experience itself, not idealism (van Kaam, 1969). Phenomenology provided just such a grounding, especially for psychology. The compartmentalizing of psychology from other disciplines in general, and other subspecialties within psychology in particular (e.g., clinical psychologists not staying current with developmental psychologists), increases the likelihood that an integration of knowledge about humans will be fragmentary, at best. This needs to change, and the cognitive and constructivist theorists are trying to do just that, as the various chapters in this book demonstrate. Yet, there are still some conceptual holes that need to be addressed, and I think the following may be why.

Psychology, for far too long, has been too busy explaining what it thinks is happening, not what people actually experience as happening. Hence, research such as Zachar (2000) cites tremendous distance between people's reports of what they experience and what psychologists theorize keeps reoccurring. More attention needs to be paid to experience, not theory, and a paradigmatic shift is badly needed. Psychology forms theories, and these theories are then used to interpret experience. It is much more beneficial to articulate experience itself, and therefore start with more detailed descriptions of experience, which can then coalesce into theories. If we start from experience, some holes in our already existing theories become clearer.

COGNITIVE PSYCHOLOGY'S HOLES

In my opinion, the following are a few holes we need to begin addressing. What we seem to do is move ahead in our clinical and research work as if these problems did not exist, as Zachar (2000) has noted. Long before Zachar, there was Husserl, Heidegger, Sartre, Merleau-Ponty, and others, who tried to redirect the flow of intellectual thinking in these areas. In philosophy, they did, but, with the exception of Adler and other existential or existentially oriented thinkers (e.g., Rollo May, Abraham Maslow, Gordon Allport, Irvin Yalom, or Adrian van Kaam, among others), mainstream psychology did not pay too much attention. With the cognitive revolution, some of their concepts seeped back in, often without recognition or acknowledgment, with works such as the Dreyfus and Hall (1982) volume and the van Kaam (1969) program model being notable exceptions. With constructionist theories, they have come back in very strongly, and Jones and Lyddon even cite Husserl (1913/1962). The absorption of these concepts has not been consistent, however, and therefore some holes exist. The six areas I would like to focus on next reveal some of the more key issues.

Self or Style

Cognitive theorists have tended to place the self as the center of control. Adler (1956) was wary of this; instead, he referred to the individual's style of life. The style was more the locus of control. The self as the origin and center of an individual's functioning is coming back into fashion, yet, as the phenomenologists have attempted to demonstrate, the self is regularly an end product of the individual's movement through life, not an initiator. If this one assumption is valid, a number of other constructs begin to become rather untenable. For example, I do not find myself thinking, "I will write these words": I simply write them. Concert pianists do not think about what they are playing: They simply play. Awareness of self comes after performance, not during or before (Sartre, 1936/1957). Ah yes, some say, but simply because you are aware of yourself after the fact does not mean that the self does not initiate the action, with awareness coming afterwards. Well, not quite, as I try to explain next.

Cognition or Consciousness

Somewhere in the 1950s, with the rise of behaviorism, the term *consciousness* fell out of vogue. *Cognition* became more acceptable, because it somehow seemed more scientific, and therefore more measurable. But what exactly is cognition? If cognition is defined as thinking (Reber, 1985), there are some major conceptual difficulties. In everyday clinical usage, these difficulties are not particularly relevant, but as research into cognition grows, several holes in the concept appear, especially if the notion of self is no longer placed as central, as the aforementioned phenomenologists discovered. Thinking has too often been equated with linguistic processing. That is not only too narrow an association, it may be flatly wrong. As work on multiple intelligences has gained in sophistication, clinicians and theorists have become aware that many people can be thinking without being linguistically engaged in a task (Flanagan, Genshaft, & Harrison, 1997). If the term *consciousness* is used instead, the matter becomes clearer. People can intend to do many things without having to think them. *Intentionality* is the more useful concept, as the phenomenologists and recent cognitive scientists have detailed (Dreyfus & Hall, 1982). As they have written, consciousness is what it intends, or put another way, what people intend becomes consciousness. Given that, therefore, what most theorists refer to as cognition might be more accurately described as *reflection*.

Cognition or Reflection

Reflection is the process whereby individuals become aware of themselves and their projects. When they become aware, it is because their intentions have failed to actualize. I am not aware of using a pen, unless the pen runs out of ink. Similarly, I am not aware I want someone's attention, unless I am not getting it. Failure of intentional structures leads to a shift in consciousness, from nonreflective to reflective (van Kaam, 1969). What many theorists describe as *unconscious* really means nonreflective: We simply do not reflect upon what our intentions are. We are still conscious of them, but simply conscious of them without reflecting upon them. With a concept such as *reflection*, we can avoid some confusing (and at times nonsensical) terminology, such as "unconscious thinking." If the self is not the center or locus of control, but consciousness exists through the intentional structures of the style, we can be conscious of something without having to reflect (i.e., think) about it. All of this leads to the next point.

Cognition and Perception

Traditionally, cognitively oriented theorists have declared that cognition determines perception. Again, in clinical usage (i.e., on a functional level), that is quite helpful. However, it is conceptually inaccurate. Research that attempts to find such a connection will fall into the kinds of traps Merleau-Ponty (1946/1962) so minutely detailed. Perception underlies cognition; it does not follow it. It cannot. Since consciousness is consciousness of something, consciousness is always "in the world" (to use a classic existential phrase). This keyboard does not fill the empty space of my consciousness; my consciousness is this keyboard and the words being written. What I perceive is my consciousness. If I thought and then I saw, there would be a gap not only in concepts, but also in time: Yet there is never a time when we do not perceive, even if it is our own consciousness (on a peripheral level). We perceive even when we do not reflect or deliberate (with imagination being a special type of consciousness I do not want to discuss at this time). We can reflect or not; we cannot not perceive. Perception is the superordinate concept. It is fundamental to consciousness and, in many ways, synonymous with it.

Perspective and the Concept of the Body

If perception is the key concept, and not cognition, how do we explain the origin of perception? Psychologists have relied upon the notion of sensation. As the phenomenologists have detailed, this cannot work. In fact, *sensation* is not a fundamental concept; it is a higher-order abstraction. Sensation implies a starting point—that there is a time without something, then sensations come rushing in. We always perceive. Perceptions may shift, but they do not begin. The field shifts, but never "starts." What about being in a silent room, and then music starts? Is there not a moment of nothing, then something? No. Even silence has a sound. Perhaps we are even hearing our own heartbeat via the blood rushing through the circulatory system of the inner ear, but we are still hearing something. If this is so, then the concept of sensation is an abstraction, not a fundamental starting point. And if this is so, then all perception is perception from a vantage point, a *perspective*. The perspective may shift, but the perceptions are ongoing, because our bodies exist in a world and always will, as long as we live. We are embodied beings, and having a body implies a focus from a perspective. Our bodies exist in three dimensions: That is a fact of existence. When cognitive scientists attempt to explain cognition without reference to the body and the perspective it opens us up to, they are operating as if we are disembodied beings. Consciousness exists through perceptions, and perceptions are perceptions from a perspective, and a perspective is fundamental to being human and the product of having a body that exists in space and time. A magnifying glass only illuminates what is placed under it. We are not so very different. We are conscious only of what we intend, and we intend only what our bodies actualize (or more precisely, attempt to actualize).

Posture and the Body and the Notion of Style Revisited

We are back to the first point. The body exists in space and time, and through its movements and actions learning occurs (Piaget, 1964/1967). It is there because of our style, our way of moving through the world. Our intentions are revealed to us via our perceptions, which are a product of our perspective. Our perspective reveals a posture, an attitudinal stance toward what is seen. For example, my posture, or, in psychological language, my attitude, toward a particular piece of music, will be revealed to me almost instantaneously. I will then reflect upon my bodily reaction and determine "I don't like this piece." The cognition, "I don't like this," did not come before my attitude; my attitude revealed my intention, which then helped determine my cognition.

How does all this translate into something more sequential and comprehensible? I attempt to outline that next. Sequentially displayed, the series I am outlining looks like this:

1. The body (or style, in Adlerian language)
2. has (or more accurately, is) a perspective
3. that opens it up to a perceptual field
4. which is a product of intentions (or goals, in Adlerian language)
5. that we are only aware of upon reflection
6. when the intentions fail to actualize.
7. It is then that we may become aware of ourselves.
8. In our awareness, we then attempt to reconstruct the entire process as if the self (7 above) came first (1 above).
9. We then construct beliefs about a central agency initiating the above sequence, often with ad hoc explanations stating that we knowingly and deliberately did such and such.

What does this sequence mean in relation to cognition? Cognitions do not start the sequence, because they cannot. Hence the title of this chapter, "A Cognitive Conundrum." The only way out of such a conundrum is to broaden the definition of cognition until it means almost anything, which is exactly what we have done. It leads to a blind alley in which everything is called a cognition, and therefore nothing is explained. If cognition is a product of the mind only, yet also an initiator, then we are in a loop of causality that gets us nowhere. The concept of intention is more likely to lead us to an answer.

Sartre (1943/1956) discussed, in philosophical language, being-in-itself and being-for-itself. Being-in-itself simply is, as in points 1–6; it is not conscious nor is it nonconscious. Being-for-itself is conscious, in the manner discussed above, in points 7–9. Being-in-itself lives its projects, its intentions. Intentions, in true Piagetian fashion, are sensorimotor-like operations. They build structures without the subject necessarily having awareness of the structures themselves. Although intentions are sensorimotor in origin and function, they are dynamically driven to facilitate adaptation or, in Sartre's language, to facilitate the goals of the fundamental project of the being-in-itself. In more commonsense language, intentions are lived and therefore experienced, not thought about in any linguistic manner. Intentions are found in actions, not in cognitions. We do not know our intentions; we discover them after the fact. They leave their footprints, in terms of structures. Cognition then comes afterwards, to explain what has already happened. Cognitively oriented theorists have tended to reverse the experiential sequence.

These structures permeate the body (or style), because their expression and mode of adaptation is through the body, through sensorimotor application and integration. Hands, eyes, ears, lips, fingers, skin—all of these parts (and more) are the interface between the body and the mind, or, in Sartre's (1943/1956) language, the being-for-itself. The body interacts with the world through these (and other) body parts. Cognitions generally do not direct the hands; the hands are way ahead of the brain in activities such as typing or piano playing. If this is the case in relatively basic but complex functions like typing or piano playing, one can see how really complex social behavior becomes. Cognitions are no more directive there than in more basic or simple functions like driving.

If intentions permeate the body, and, hence, the posture—the openness—to life, perceptions become more readily understandable. We can only perceive that which we are open to, and that may be a foregone conclusion. My scanning the perceptual field will be linked to my perspective, and my perspective is already determined by the placement of my body, before I am reflectively aware of what I am perceiving. This was Merleau-Ponty's (1946/1962, 1960/1964) point when he argued for both the phenomenology and primacy of perception. My noticing a book out of place on the shelf is already an indication of a bias to seek out such things; once they are seen, I then come to the awareness that something is out of place. The perceptual experience nonreflectively preceded the cognition and linguistic formulation. In fact, it set the stage for the cognition itself. It could only set the stage for such a cognition, because the body had gone into the room, faced the bookshelves, scanned the books, and opened itself up to the intention to find something wrong. Hence, the proofreader's ability to find mistakes the author misses. The author did not intend to find them, but the proofreader did.

CONCLUSION

As we begin to move away from the overly simplistic notions of the behaviorists or the reductionism of the biologically oriented theorists who want to ground all psychology in neurology or physiology, we are left with having to explain what people actually experience (Zachar, 2000). The aforementioned six points, and subsequent detailing of them, have been implied since (at least) 1844, in Soren Kierkegaard's work, and almost simultaneously in Friedrich Nietzsche's work. The cognitive theorists in general, and the constructionists in particular, have made, in my opinion, the most refreshing inroads in this area since the phenomenologists. Adler (1956) declared that the style determines the person and what the person perceives, thinks, and even remembers. However, Adler never articulated this in the kind of detail that lent itself to the rigorous empirical or conceptual investigation needed to explain what exactly this means. The phenomenologists did, but their work is being read only by philosophers, and sometimes only by existential philosophers. The constructionists have rediscovered Vaihinger, and, as has been detailed by many, Vaihinger was a key source for Adler (1911/2002). Vaihinger was a neo-Kantian. In other words, his work was looking to expand upon the conceptualizations of Immanuel Kant, the German philosopher who so dominated European thinking in the nineteenth and early twentieth centuries. Kant's work was brilliant, and his conceptualizations were foundational for not only Vaihinger and Adler, but also for Husserl, and Husserl taught Heidegger, Sartre, and Merleau-Ponty. These thinkers have expanded, elaborated, and, in many instances, pushed Kant's overly cognitive formulations further than Vaihinger and, therefore, have opened many doors that Vaihinger left closed (Dreyfus & Hall, 1982).

As the constructionists adopt a language and conceptual system taken over from Vaihinger/Kant, they are likely to run into the same roadblocks Husserl discovered in his investigations, which were then tackled, and in some ways resolved, by his disciples. If some of the formulations I present in this admittedly short chapter can call attention to some of their relatively newer concepts, perhaps we can avoid yet another modification of an already existing wheel. Perhaps then psychology can stop defending itself against attack and instead continue to grow and integrate with the other sciences and disciplines. Dialogues such as those found in this book are magnificent and badly needed, but now the dialogue needs to expand to other disciplines and areas, including philosophy. Hopefully, this chapter can point to one additional, possible area that it must explore: the actual, lived, experience of people. It is there where our attention—and theorizing—must go.

REFERENCES

Adler, A. (1956). *The Individual Psychology of Alfred Adler* (H. L. Ansbacher & R. R. Ansbacher, Eds.). New York: Basic Books.

Adler, A. (2002). *The neurotic character: Fundamentals of Individual Psychology and psychotherapy* (C. Koen, Trans., & H. Stein, Ed.). San Francisco: Alfred Adler Institute of San Francisco. (Original work published 1911)

Dreyfus, H. L., & Hall, H. (Eds.). (1982). *Husserl, intentionality, and cognitive science.* Cambridge, MA: MIT Press.

Flanagan, D. P., Genshaft, J. L., & Harrison, P. L. (Eds.). (1997). *Contemporary intellectual assessment: Theories, tests, and issues.* New York: Guilford Press.

Gopnik, A., Meltzoff, A. N., & Kuhl, P. K. (1999). *The scientist in the crib: Minds, brains, and how children learn.* New York: William Morrow.

Grigsby, J., & Stevens, D. (2000). *Neurodynamics of personality.* New York: Guilford Press.

Heidegger, M. (1962). *Being and time* (J. Macquarrie & E. Robinson, Trans.). New York: Harper & Row. (Original work published 1927)

Heidegger, M. (1968). *What is called thinking?* (J. Glenn Gray, Trans.). New York: Harper & Row. (Original work published 1954)

Hergenhahn, B. R. (1997). *An introduction to the history of psychology* (3rd ed.). New York: Brooks/Cole Publishing.

Husserl, E. (1962). *Ideas: General introduction to pure phenomenology* (W. R. Boyce Gibson, Trans.). New York: Collier Books. (Original work published 1913)

Husserl, E. (1970). *The crisis of European sciences and transcendental phenomenology* (D. Carr, Trans.). Evanston, IL: Northwestern University Press. (Original lectures 1937)

Ihde, D. (1977). *Experimental phenomenology: An introduction.* New York: Paragon Books.

Ihde, D. (1993). *Postphenomenology: Essays in the postmodern context.* Evanston, IL: Northwestern University Press.

Joseph, R. (1992). *The right brain and the unconscious: Discovering the stranger within.* New York: Plenum Press.

Kierkegaard, S. (1980). *The concept of anxiety: A simple psychologically orienting deliberation on the dogmatic issue of hereditary sin* (R. Thomte in collaboration with A. B. Anderson, Trans.). Princeton, NJ: Princeton University Press. (Original work published 1844)

Merleau-Ponty, M. (1962). *The phenomenology of perception* (C. Smith, Trans.). New Jersey: Humanities Press/Routledge & Kegan Paul. (Original work published 1946)

Merleau-Ponty, M. (1964). The child's relation with others (W. Cobb, Trans.). In M. Merleau-Ponty, *The primacy of perception: And other essays on phenomenological psychology, the philosophy of art, history and politics* (J. M. Edie, Ed.) (pp. 96–155). Evanston, IL: Northwestern University Press. (Original work published 1960)

Mosak, H., & Maniacci, M. (1999). *A primer of Adlerian psychology: The analytic-behavioral-cognitive psychology of Alfred Adler.* Philadelphia: Brunner/Mazel.

Nietzsche, F. (1967). *The will to power* (W. Kaufmann & R. J. Hollingdale, Trans.; W. Kaufmann, Ed.). New York: Random House. (Original work published 1901)

Piaget, J. (1967). *Six psychological studies* (A. Tenzer, Trans., & D. Elkind, Ed.). New York: Random House. (Original work published 1964)

Reber, A. S. (1985). *The Penguin dictionary of psychology.* New York: Penguin.

Sartre, J-P. (1956). *Being and nothingness* (H. Barnes, Trans.). New York: Gramercy Books. (Original work published 1943)

Sartre, J-P. (1957). *The transcendence of the ego: An existentialist theory of consciousness* (F. Williams & R. Kirkpatrick, Trans.). New York: Farrar, Straus and Giroux. (Original work published 1936)

van Kaam, A. (1969). *Existential foundations of psychology.* New York: Image Books/Doubleday.

Zachar, P. (2000). *Psychological concepts and biological psychiatry: A philosophical analysis.* Philadelphia: John Benjamins.

8
Two Paths Diverge in a Wood: Cognitive–Constructivist Contrasts and the Future Evolution of Adlerian Psychotherapy

Robert A. Neimeyer

I began reading the foregoing chapters, by Watts and Shulman, Jones and Lyddon, Sperry, and Freeman and Urschel, with something like the blend of excitement and anxiety that might accompany the anticipation of a family reunion involving the far-flung members of a sprawling kinship network. Whether constructivism is regarded as the prodigal progeny of Adlerian theory, or whether the two approaches represent kissing cousins with a different set of first-degree relatives, I suspected that there would be no denying the family resemblance. I therefore found myself looking forward to the sharing of mutual memories of common ancestors and the animated exchange of stories recounting where our respective paths in life had taken us. Like all such anticipations, this one carried with it a shade of uncertainty—how compatible would we really be at deep levels, and could we understand and respect each other?—but, primarily, I looked forward to the conversation and the deepening of relational bonds that was likely to result.

At first, my hoped-for expectation of intriguing interactions was not disappointed. Listening in on the reunion conversations of the first two sets of authors, I could not help but be struck by their similarity in voice as well as values, and looking through the snapshots of Adlerian and constructivist lineages that each passed around made it clear that they shared a common intellectual inheritance. At the same time, different family members exemplified different strengths: Some were practical, others more abstract; some social, others more individualistic. However, these divergent styles seemed to be built on convergent commitments to respect, humility, and interest in the viability of perspectives different from their own. This, I thought, was what a family reunion should be at its best, offering the possibility of relational reconnection and the prospect of continued conversation among people who had enough in common to make cooperation possible, and enough distinctness to make collaboration profitable. Even if the future prospects for a more integrated family system could only be indistinctly glimpsed in the dusty crystal ball, I found myself looking forward to furthering the conversation.

But gradually, as I shifted to the other two tables, a darkening shadow of doubt began to spread over the whole enterprise. Not only did these more cognitive speakers carry a different accent, but they also seemed driven by a discernibly different set of concerns than those that had animated the earlier conversations. To make matters more confusing, the speakers seemed to be in the same general line of work as their presumptive relatives at the other tables, but their way of approaching it made it clear that they had attended very different trade schools, or at least learned rather different lessons. Not that they were unsuccessful in their respective career paths (if anything, their tailored appearance suggested that their services were widely sought after), but, rather, their technical fascination with the tools of their trade suggested a fundamentally different orientation to those they served than was implicit in the earlier Adlerian–constructivist conversations. Listening to their enthusiastic banter was entertaining enough at one level, but I found myself politely edging away from the cognitive strategizing to seek refuge in the company of my earlier compatriots. How, I wondered, would these two branches of the family get along, and would intermarriage between them have the same prospects of success as that between the Montagues and Capulets?

This chapter is essentially a personal meditation on the aforementioned question. It begins with a brief exploration of what might be meant by *integration* of different theoretical traditions, then considers whether and where in the proposed merger of Adlerian, constructivist, and cognitive therapies such a coming-together might be achievable and advisable.

EPISTEMOLOGY AND THE PROBLEM OF INTEGRATION

The *Concise Oxford Dictionary* (1999) defines *integration* as "the act of completing by bringing together parts into a whole." This succinct definition carries at least three implications. The first is that integration is an act, a process undertaken over time. By inference, it is accomplished only gradually, rather than abruptly or by fiat. The second implication is that this process entails some sort of bringing together of parts, suggesting visually that each of the parts is in some sense brought closer to the other. In this respect, integration implies something different than the mere subordination of some parts to others. And finally, this definition implies that the resulting unity is more whole or complete than its constituents. On this criterion, the integrated entity would be holistic, rather than a fragmentary concatenation of conflicting parts. How does the proposed integration of Adlerian, constructivist, and cognitive approaches to psychotherapy fare in terms of the implicit requirements of this definition?

To address this question, it is helpful to consider what might be meant by integration in the context of psychotherapy—a topic that has received intensive attention in the past 15 years (Goldfried, 1995; Norcross, 1986). What emerge are multiple answers, put forth by different constituencies, each of which differs importantly in its aims as well as its methods (R. A. Neimeyer, 1993). At the least ambitious end of the continuum, integration might simply mean *technical eclecticism*, tolerating or encouraging the therapist's adopting whatever works, or seems to work, in assisting a given client (Whitaker & Keith, 1981). Although common in practice, it is rarely advocated by psychotherapy scholars and researchers. The unsystematic penchant to borrow any superficially attractive technique, in the absence of orienting principles or heuristics, leaves the therapist rudderless in the often uncharted waters of psychotherapeutic process—interpreting transference patterns at one moment, disputing irrational thoughts at another, and using paradoxical interventions at a third. Indeed, it was the common recourse to mere technical eclecticism, as the simplest apparent alternative to being "stuck" in a single, tradition-bound school of therapy, which gave rise to the field of psychotherapy integration in the first place, in an attempt to benefit from some of its flexibility, without succumbing to its obvious limitations.

A second attempt to increase the flexibility of therapeutic practice takes the form of a variation on this theme. In *systematic eclecticism*, the therapist selects an approach—such as directive, behavioral interventions or more exploratory, emotion-focused work—depending on the characteristics of the client, such as his or her degree of psychological reactance to being controlled by another, or tendency to construe life problems in externalizing or internalizing terms (Beutler & Clarkin, 1990). Although the attempt to inform therapist intuition about what to use when, with data-based predictions, is commendable, evidence concerning the effectiveness of this matching orientation is equivocal (Baker & Neimeyer, 2003). More fundamentally, it could be claimed that even a successful program of systematic technical eclecticism would represent not so much a form of psychotherapy *integration* as a form of *systematic pluralism*, permitting more-informed switching between orientations, without promoting their assimilation into a larger, more coherent, conceptual framework.

A third, more serious path toward integration has been blazed by *common factors* theorists. Those associated with this perspective argue that it is not what distinguishes various approaches to therapy that makes them effective, but what they hold in common that matters—factors like the development of a strong therapeutic relationship, the cultivation of hope, and the use of credible rituals that engender the client's faith that change is possible (Arkowitz, 1992). Proponents of this view find support in the essential equivalence of effectiveness of different approaches, both for specific disorders like depression (Robinson, Berman, & Neimeyer, 1990) and for the broad range of problems for which people seek therapeutic help (Luborsky et al., 2002). Moreover, clearly, such common factors as the client–therapist relationship account for significant portions of the variance in outcome, irrespective of the particular techniques on which the therapists rely (Messer & Wampold, 2002). Nonetheless, it seems unlikely that common factors shared by all forms of helping are exhaustive in accounting for psychotherapeutic change, because studies point to the additional importance of technical factors and subtle features of the interaction between therapists and their chosen methods in mediating outcome (Baker & Neimeyer, in press). Therefore, seeking the integration of different approaches, by reducing them to factors accounting only for their shared variance, would appear to risk contracting therapeutic practice, rather than expanding it. Stated differently, common factors may be necessary, but not sufficient, ingredients of an expanded model of psychotherapy.

Finally, and most ambitiously, some psychotherapy scholars have advocated true *theoretical integration*, whereby two or more different approaches to psychotherapy would be merged to form a more encompassing theory of human problems and principles of change (Wachtel, 1991). The bringing together of originally distinct behavioral and cognitive therapies into a hybrid cognitive-behavioral model reflects one such integration, yielding an offspring theory that is arguably more comprehensive and technically diverse than either of its parents considered alone. However, it seems clear that not all candidate theories are equally amenable to mergers of this kind: What kind of hybrid would result from the cross-fertilization of psychodynamic approaches, emphasizing intrapsychic conflict, with strategic therapies focusing on interaction sequences within families? Thus, the promise of psychotherapy integration at this conceptual level can only be realized if principles are identified that assist in the identification of candidate theories that can contribute coherently to a more overarching theoretical framework (Messer, 1987).

As a step in this direction, I have elsewhere sketched the outlines of an approach I have termed *theoretically progressive integration*, or TPI (R. A. Neimeyer, 1993; Neimeyer & Feixas, 1990). At the heart of this perspective is a concern with epistemological criteria for integration, criteria concerned with the basic approaches to knowledge that shape the various theories to be integrated. In this view, each system of psychotherapy embodies a distinctive set of epistemological commitments, ranging from core, often implicit, metatheoretical beliefs about the nature of reality and human beings' relationship to that reality, through formal theories of human functioning and clinical theories of the nature of human distress and disorder, to therapeutic strategies and techniques (see Figure 8.1). Such a multilevel view of psychotherapeutic theorizing accords with contemporary models of the structure of scientific research programs more generally, which are viewed as organized around a hard core of metatheoretical commitments that are typically defended against refutation, although more peripheral aspects of the theory might be modified in response to empirical research (Lakatos, 1974). By implication, the ideal candidate approaches for psychotherapy integration would be two different models of therapy that showed strong convergence at core levels, but considerable diversity at strategic levels, offering the twin advantages of conceptual coherence and technical expansion when merged into a more comprehensive model. A fuller exposition of the details of the TPI model is provided elsewhere (R. A. Neimeyer, 1993).

Two Paths Diverge in a Wood   127

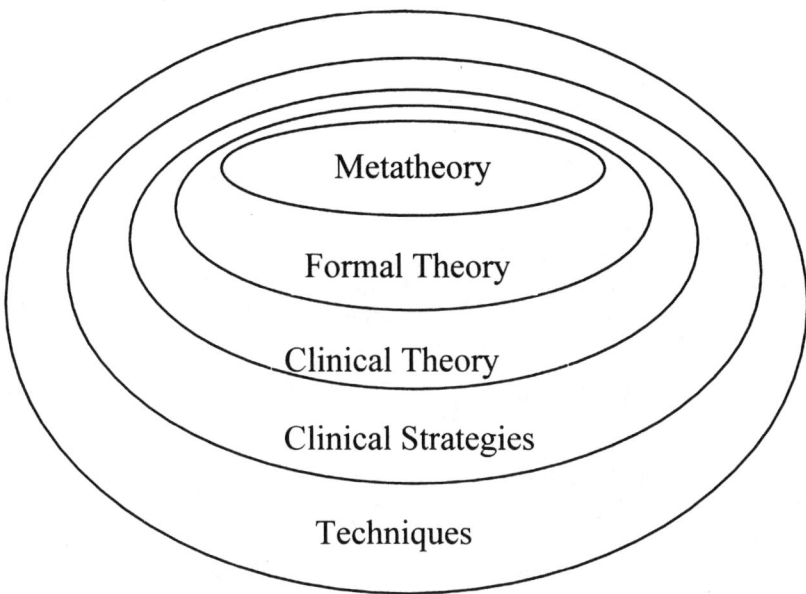

FIGURE 8.1   Epistemological structure of psychotherapy theories.

REFLECTIONS ON THE PRESENT INTEGRATIVE DIALOGUE

How do the proposed integrations of Adlerian therapy on the one hand, and constructivist and cognitive therapies on the other, fare, in these terms? In a word, the answer is, differently. Table 8.1 presents a list of the epistemological commitments of Adlerian, constructivist, and cognitive therapies as described by the contributors to this volume, classed by structural level: metatheory, formal theory, clinical theory, and strategies and techniques. Several observations at each of these levels immediately compel attention, from the standpoint of the contemplated merger of the three orientations.

First, both Adlerian and constructivist scholars carefully explicate their core metatheoretical commitments to a view of human beings as creative, proactive, participatory agents in the construction of their own experience, orienting toward fictional goals that cannot be meaningfully adjudicated in terms of their simple validity. Instead, the overarching frameworks of meaning that people construct can be evaluated only in

TABLE 8.1 Epistemological Commitments of Adlerian, Constructivist, and Cognitive Therapies

Epistemological commitment	Adlerian therapy	Constructivist therapy	Cognitive therapy
Metatheory	Human beings as creative, goal-directed agents, the "artists" of their own personalities	Human beings are proactive, anticipatory participants in configuring their perceptions and knowing.	
	Fictional goals taken as truth; meanings of world created rather than intrinsic	Constructions are fictional, "as if" creations; cannot be assessed in terms of correspondence with objective reality	Maladaptive schemas distort reality.
	Functionalist emphasis; focus on psychology of use	Combined functionalist–structuralist emphasis; focus on evolution of construct system	
Formal theory	People develop their unique life story or lifestyle, an abstract principle for organizing the content of experience.	Individuality is shaped by our personal construct systems, self-narratives, core ordering processes	
		Intense emotion is entailed in core change, adaptive; not problem to be 'cured'	
	Personality is a unity, an integrated whole.	Selfhood is holistic, coherent, favoring consistency, maintenance.	

TABLE 8.1 *(continued)*

Epistemological commitment	Adlerian therapy	Constructivist therapy	Cognitive therapy
	Lifestyle, goals, and core convictions typically out of awareness	Core ordering processes are tacit or unconscious.	
	Communal realities are socially constructed; family constellation shapes style of life and social interest.	Organizing processes reflect and influence social systems; attachment shapes model of subject and object.	
Clinical theory	Failure to develop social interest leads to movement against/away from others.	Problems in forming attachment or dependency relationships contribute to disturbed models of self and other.	Intrapsychic definition of pathology, but internalization of early relationship schema plays important role.
	Disorders best understood as demoralization, rather than diagnoses.	Diagnoses are eschewed in order to focus on limitations imposed by previous life narratives.	Disorders diagnosed and researched in DSM terms, classifying clients as suffering from depressive, anxiety, and personality disorders.
	Symptoms are "solutions" chosen because they are perceived as facilitating goals.	Symptoms are coherent with core constructs; suggest constraints of the system	Maladaptive schemas of self, world, and others generate manifest problems.
	Compensation is an attempt to safeguard lifestyle convictions that are being challenged.	Resistance to change arises when core ordering processes are threatened and no alternatives are available.	

(continued)

TABLE 8.1 *(continued)*

Epistemological commitment	Adlerian therapy	Constructivist therapy	Cognitive therapy
Clinical strategies	Therapeutic relationship empathic, egalitarian, modeling social interest	Therapeutic relationship empathic, respectful, even reverential, offering secure base	Therapist plays directive role in treatment conceptualization, collaboration, and planning.
	Preference for qualitative, idiographic assessment in course of therapy	Preference for qualitative, idiographic assessment in course of therapy	Agenda established through discrete problem list and "objective" quantitative measures
	Change requires gaining insight into schema of apperception, basic convictions, style of life.	Change occurs as people question, deconstruct, and reconstruct their own realities.	Change involves reorienting client's cognitive and behavioral skills and goals.
	Encouragement of client to draw on assets, focus on progress	Emphasis on client strengths and resources	Emphasis on clients' cognitive distortions and basic skill deficits, as well as their erroneous views of these skills
	Therapy is process of encouragement, not cure.	Inquisitive, "curious" stance toward client constructions	Socratic search for "basic mistakes" and "faulty assumptions" in client schema

TABLE 8.1 *(continued)*

Epistemological commitment	Adlerian therapy	Constructivist therapy	Cognitive therapy
Techniques	Birth-order analysis Acting "as if" Magic wand Prescribing the symptom The question Task-setting Lifestyle analysis Early recollections Public education Spitting in the soup Push-button technique Dream analysis	Repertory grids Fixed-role therapy Self-narratives Mirror time dialogue Streaming Novelty moderation Attachment analysis	Implosion Flooding Modeling Operant conditioning Cognitive rehearsal Cognitive restructuring Desensitization Behavior modification Idiosyncratic meaning Reattribution De-catastrophizing Guided discovery Thought stopping Distraction Direct disputation Labeling distortions Activity scheduling Assertion training In vivo exposure Bibliotherapy

functional terms concerned with their viability for those who live by them. By contrast, cognitive therapy is relatively silent about its basic metatheoretical epistemology, except in emphasizing the supposedly distorting role of "maladaptive" schemas, with its implicit criterion of degree of "reality contact," in distinguishing between "healthy" and "unhealthy" beliefs. At a general level, this contrast implies a rather different attitude toward client realities, with Adlerians and constructivists adopting a more credulous, curious, or even celebratory stance; cognitive therapists view these same constructions with some suspicion. These divergent metatheories—one adopting a coherence theory of truth, the other a correspondence theory (Neimeyer, 1995)—suggest different interventions at strategic and technical levels, as noted below.

The contrasts between Adlerian and constructivist approaches on the one hand and cognitive therapy on the other are equally striking at the level of their respective formal theories of human functioning. In keeping with their intent to provide comprehensive theories of personality and social behavior, both of the former perspectives offer detailed and strongly converging images of human nature, enunciating the basis of individuality in lifestyle, stressing the integral, coherent construction of selfhood, noting the limits of awareness in accessing and symbolizing core processes and convictions, and situating personal identity solidly in the context of interpersonal relationships. The depiction of cognitive therapy, on the other hand, again falls silent regarding these theoretical foundations, suggesting its more limited scope as a clinical theory divorced from a broader, philosophically informed view of human functioning. Although the failure of cognitive therapists to articulate a broad-reaching theory of personality might not preclude some form of integration with the other approaches, neither does it provide an argument for their paradigmatic compatibility, making all the more crucial an assessment of the goodness of fit of the various approaches at the level of clinical theory.

And yet, important discrepancies arise at the level of clinical theory, as well. Constructivist and Adlerian approaches strongly ground disturbances in social interest or role construction in the matrix of the social world; cognitive therapy offers a principally intrapsychic definition of distress, although with growing acknowledgment that early relationships must play some role in shaping problematic self-schemas. More tellingly, the discernable reluctance of Adlerians and constructivists to pathologize human experience, through the use of classificatory psychiatric diagnoses, stands in sharp juxtaposition to cognitive therapy's traditional reliance on the very diagnostic labels (e.g., depression, anxiety disorder, personality disorder) eschewed by the other two approaches. This is further reflected in the Adlerian and constructivist conceptualization of symptoms as congruent with core goals and constructs, manifesting a systemic coherence with the person's overall style of life, which leads to understandable resistance to change when such constructions are threatened in therapy. This inside view of the structure and function of clinical problems is replaced by a mostly external perspective in cognitive therapy, which underscores the maladaptive quality of client schemas, as judged by the therapist, or presumed extrinsic criteria, such as degree of match with reality. Accordingly, this leads to strikingly different modal differences in intervention strategies, as noted below.

How do the various orientations converge or diverge at the level of clinical strategies? As a perusal of Table 8.1 indicates, constructivist and Adlerian approaches are characterized by very similar styles of work, predicated on an empathic, respectful, and curious stance toward client meanings, which are assessed through a variety of chiefly qualitative, idiographic interview procedures. From this perspective, therapists are enjoined to follow the client's central concerns, heightening their awareness of the implications of their core convictions, goals, and constructions, and providing encouragement for experimenting with new insights in practical life contexts. Therapy draws mostly on clients' strengths and competencies, in a solution-focused, rather than problem-focused, fashion.

By contrast, cognitive therapy is portrayed by its enthusiasts as therapist-directed, both in conceptualization and treatment planning, measuring clients on the nomothetic yardsticks of conventional psychiatric symptomatology and dysfunction. Likewise, cognitive assessment seeks to identify the client's "basic mistakes," "cognitive errors," and "skill deficits," providing remediation for these presumed deficits through systematic instruction in a variety of approved techniques. As such, it is problem-focused and diagnostic, relying on Socratic questioning for revealing the faulty assumptions from which the client purportedly suffers. And, like the Socrates of Plato's *Republic*, cognitive therapists are supported by the conviction that their goal is to dispel the shadows of delusion and error that characterize the thinking of those with whom they are in dialogue. Significantly, such a depiction of the therapeutic relationship is at sharp variance with those offered by the constructivist and Adlerian theorists contributing to this volume.

Finally, at the level of specific therapeutic techniques, cognitive and constructivist procedures again give the impression of being sampled from different populations of procedures. The illustrative constructivist methods mentioned by the authors, like the broader set of techniques they represent (Mahoney, 1991; G. J. Neimeyer, 1993; Neimeyer & Raskin, 2001), tend to provide opportunities for client self-reflection on core themes and meanings (e.g., mirror time, repertory grids, narrative procedures) or contexts for engagement in novel experiential learning (e.g., stream of consciousness methods, fixed-role therapy). Methods preferred by cognitive therapists, on the other hand, are conspicuously more directive, being targeted toward designated behavior change (e.g., implosion, flooding, modeling, behavior modification, assertion training) or cognitive retraining (e.g., thought-stopping, labeling distortions, cognitive disputation, rehearsal, restructuring). Taken as a whole, each set of procedures is fully coherent, with a constructivist or cognitive emphasis, respectively, on therapy as a means of heightening client reflexivity and self-directed exploration, or as a set of therapist-specified procedures for remediating client skill deficits and cognitive dysfunctions.

By comparison, Adlerian techniques incline toward a constructivist emphasis on exploratory, "as if" engagement with the client's reality (e.g., the question, early recollections, dream analysis, acting hypothetically), although some more directive procedures also are advocated (e.g., prescribing the symptom, task-setting, public education). From the standpoint of a theoretically progressive integration of models, however, a "Chinese menu" eclecticism (choosing one technique from column A, another from column B, and a third from column C) would seem likely to produce an indiscriminate gallimaufry of therapeutic methods, in the absence of convergent conceptualization. (Imagine the eager therapist delicately teasing out the core commitments of the client's lifestyle or the central themes of the client's self-narrative at one point, only to label their distortions and dispute their idiosyncratic logic the next.)

The above observations regarding the parallels of Adlerian and constructivist approaches at the levels of metatheory, formal theory, clinical theory, and even clinical strategy, relative to the contrasts of both approaches with cognitive therapy at each of these levels, suggest that a progressive integration of the former two traditions could be as propitious as a merger with the latter would be precarious. Indeed, the well-intentioned proposal to integrate cognitive and narrative approaches (Ramsay, 1998) has recently encountered similar epistemological and practical problems (Neimeyer, 1998).

CONCLUSIONS

What do the foregoing considerations imply about the feasibility of integrating Adlerian with constructivist or cognitive approaches? Bearing in mind the Oxford definition of *integration* offered earlier—the act of completing by bringing together parts into a whole—it is clear that such a process will be a gradual one, involving selective rather than indiscriminate melding, with the goal of developing a more comprehensive, holistic system of psychotherapy than either of the parent approaches taken alone. In view of the considerable conceptual compatibility of Adlerian and constructivist approaches, at levels ranging from metatheory through clinical theory, a genuine theoretical integration of models seems possible, perhaps drawing on concepts of narrative and core ordering processes, to further specify the components of lifestyle in a therapeutically useful fashion. Moreover, the technical complementarity of the two orientations suggests the fecundity of this union, broadening the scope of compatible procedures available within the combined model. Still, endorsing the favorable conditions for such cross-fertilization is only preliminary to the actual creation of a genuine hybrid theory, something that will require a good deal of further conceptual cultivation.

Integration of Adlerian and cognitive perspectives, on the other hand, is likely to be more superficial or partial, at the level of simple technical eclecticism or—if grounds for thoughtful switching between models can be articulated—systematic eclecticism. A deeper or truer integration of approaches is likely to be complicated by the relative silence of cognitive therapy about its philosophical and theoretical roots, calling into question the grafting of cognitive techniques onto an essentially Adlerian stock. Nor is it clear that a common factors approach to integrating the two would be attractive, insofar as it would entail sacrificing those distinctive processes in each therapy that fail to correspond with procedures in the other.

Which of these diverging paths will Adlerian therapy take, or will it remain cautious about either liaison, in an attempt to preserve its independence? The realistic answer to this question is, "All of the above." Psychotherapy theories do not do the integrating, but theorists and therapists do. And, like all human beings, psychotherapy scholars and practitioners have different motivations and inclinations—toward theoretical purity, profundity, or prestige—and different conceptual styles, gravitating toward the discourses of philosophy and the humanities or toward those of empiricism and science. Accordingly, it is a safe prediction that some Adlerians will jealously guard their independence, while others will enthusiastically explore conceptual and practical exchange with perspectives that offer theoretical, therapeutic, and perhaps political advantages. Returning to the family reunion metaphor with which my reflections opened, I would expect some liaisons within this widely distributed kinship system to be more serious and sustained than others, and that the occasional resulting marriages will vary in both quality and fertility. My hope is that at least some Adlerians will approach the opportunity for conceptual coupling in a reflective fashion, seeking to preserve the unique strengths of their own family system, as they open themselves to the only partly predictable process of merging it with another.

REFERENCES

Arkowitz, H. (1992). A common factors therapy for depression. In J. Norcross & M. Goldfried (Eds.), *Handbook of psychotherapy integration* (pp. 402–432). New York: Basic.

Baker, K. D., & Neimeyer, R. A. (in press). Therapist training and client characteristics as predictors of treatment response to group therapy for depression. *Psychotherapy Research*.

Beutler, L. E., & Clarkin, J. F. (1990). *Systematic treatment selection*. New York: Brunner/Mazel.

Concise Oxford Dictionary (10th ed., 1999). Oxford, UK: Oxford University Press.

Goldfried, M. R. (1995). *From cognitive-behavior therapy to psychotherapy integration*. New York: Springer.

Lakatos, I. (1974). Falsification and the methodology of scientific research programs. In I. Lakatos & A. Musgrave (Eds.), *Criticism and the growth of knowledge* (pp. 91–196). London: Cambridge University Press.

Luborsky, L., Rosenthal, R., Diguer, L., Andrusyna, T. P., Berman, J. S., Levitt, J. T., et al. (2002). The Dodo bird verdict is alive and well—mostly. *Clinical Psychology: Science and Practice, 9*, 2–12.

Mahoney, M. J. (1991). *Human change processes*. New York: Basic Books.

Messer, S. B. (1987). Can the Tower of Babel be completed? A critique of the common language proposal. *Journal of Integrative and Eclectic Psychotherapy, 6*, 195–199.

Messer, S. B., & Wampold, B. E. (2002). Let's face facts: Common factors are more potent than specific treatments. *Clinical Psychology: Science and Practice, 9*, 21–25.

Neimeyer, G. J. (1993). *Constructivist assessment: A casebook*. Newbury Park, CA: Sage.

Neimeyer, R. A. (1993). Constructivism and the problem of psychotherapy integration. *Journal of Psychotherapy Integration, 3*, 133–157.

Neimeyer, R. A. (1995). Constructivist psychotherapies: Features, foundations, and future directions. In R. A. Neimeyer & M. J. Mahoney (Eds.), *Constructivism in psychotherapy* (pp. 11–38). Washington, DC: American Psychological Association.

Neimeyer, R. A. (1998). Cognitive therapy and the narrative trend: A bridge too far? *Journal of Cognitive Psychotherapy, 12*, 57–66.

Neimeyer, R. A., & Feixas, G. (1990). Constructivist contributions to psychotherapy integration. *Journal of Integrative and Eclectic Psychotherapy, 9,* 4–20.

Neimeyer, R. A., & Raskin, J. (2001). Varieties of constructivism in psychotherapy. In K. Dobson (Ed.), *Handbook of cognitive behavioral therapy* (2nd ed., pp. 393–430). New York: Guilford.

Norcross, J. C. (1986). Eclectic psychotherapy: An introduction and overview. In J. C. Norcross (Ed.), *Handbook of eclectic psychotherapy* (pp. 3–24). New York: Brunner Mazel.

Ramsay, J. R. (1998). Postmodern cognitive therapy: Cognitions, narratives, and personal meaning-making. *Journal of Cognitive Psychotherapy, 12,* 39–55.

Robinson, L. A., Berman, J. S., & Neimeyer, R. A. (1990). Psychotherapy for the treatment of depression: A comprehensive review of controlled outcome research. *Psychological Bulletin, 108,* 30–49.

Wachtel, P. (1991). From eclecticism to synthesis: Toward a more seamless psychotherapy integration. *Journal of Psychotherapy Integration, 1,* 43–54.

Whitaker, C., & Keith, D. (1981). Symbolic-experiential therapy. In A. Gurman & D. Kniskern (Eds.), *Handbook of family therapy* (pp. 187–225). New York: Brunner/Mazel.

Index

Active schemas, 109
Activity scheduling, 84, 131
Adaptation, 46, 74
Adler, Alfred, 1–3, 17, 92
Adler, Kurt, 72
Adlerian Counseling and Psychotherapy, 64
Adlerian therapy, generally:
   characteristics of, 1–2, 9–11, 19, 59–60
   cognitive-behavioral therapy compared with, 71–86, 91–105
   cognitive therapy compared with, 59–67, 95–105, 107–120
   constructivist therapy compared with, 10–26, 38–52, 91–105
   democratic emphasis, 92
   future directions, 122–136
   integration, generally, 96
Adversity, 83
Agenda-setting, 80
Allport, Gordon, 114
Ambivalence, 19
American Counseling Association, 93
American empirical psychology, 102
American Psychological Association, 93
Analysis, in Adlerian therapy, 23
Anticipatory embodied theory, 39
Anxiety, 63, 80
Anxiety disorders, 65, 129
Apperception, 41, 61, 95
As if philosophy, 39, 44, 131, 134
Assertion training, 84, 131, 134
Assessments, 44, 50. *See specific types of assessments*
Assimilation, 74
Association for Advancement of Behavior Therapy, 93

Attachment, generally:
   analysis, 131
   insecure, 43
   problems, 129
   style, 19
   theory, 17–18, 49–50, 97, 101
Authoritarianism, 92
Automatic thoughts, 76–77, 79, 81. *See also* Thought-stopping
Autopoiesis, 13
Awareness, 117–118

Beck, Aaron, 94
Beck Anxiety Inventory (BAI), 80–81
Beck Depression Inventory-II (BDI-II), 80
Beck Hopelessness Scale, 81
Beck Scale of Suicidal Ideation, 81
Behavioral rehearsal, 84
Behavioral theory, 97
Behaviorism, 26
Behavior modification, 131, 134
Behavior therapy, 102
Being-for-itself, 118
Being-in-itself, 118
Belief system, construction of, 42–43
Bibliotherapy, 84, 131
Birth-order analysis, 131
Body:
   concept, 116–117
   posture and, 117–118
Bonding process, 18–19, 104. *See also* Attachment
Borderline personality disorder, 65
Bowlby, John, 17
Brain-behavior relationship, 108
Brief therapy, solution-focused, 9–10
Brown v. Board of Education, 29–30

139

Causality, 118
Change, generally:
  assessments, 50
  facilitation, 23–25
  resistance, 21, 100–101, 129
Chaos theory, 99
Childhood:
  core constructs/personal narratives, 28, 42
  early recollections (ERs), 41–42, 50, 66, 75–76, 131
Clarification, 64
Client-centered therapy, 92
Client-therapist relationship, see Therapeutic relationship
Clinical strategies, 127, 130, 134
Clinical theory, 127, 129, 134
Clinical/therapy issues:
  change facilitation, 23–25
  change resistance, 21
  client-therapist relationship, 21–23
  maladjustment, 19–21
Closed systems, 99
Cognition, 14, 114–115
Cognitive approach, characteristics of, 41–42
Cognitive-behavioral therapies (CBTs):
  Adlerian psychotherapy compared with, 59–61, 64–67, 70–86
  constructivism compared with, 91–105
  defined, 59
  intrapsychic focus, 97–98
  popularity of, 71
  termination, 86
  therapeutic change, 63–64
  therapeutic focus, 61–62, 74
  therapeutic relationship, 62–63
  therapeutic structure, 78–81
  therapeutic techniques, 82–86
  treatment conceptualization, 81–82
Cognitive-perceptual model, 76
Cognitive psychology, holes in, 113–119
Cognitive rehearsal, 64, 131, 134

Cognitive restructuring, 64, 77, 131, 134
Cognitive retraining, 134
Cognitive schema, 62
Cognitive shift, 64
Cognitive therapy, 2–3, 41. *See also* Cognitive-behavioral therapies (CBTs)
Cognitive triad, 76
Coherence theory, 132
Collaboration, 22, 44
Collaborative empiricism, 62–63
Collaborative relationships, 62–63
Common factors theorists, 125
Common sense, 109
Compensation, 74, 129
Concept formation, 102
Confabulation problem, 112
Confrontation, 64
Connectedness, 47
Conscious, 109. *See also* Consciousness
Conscious-unconscious dichotomy, 27
Consciousness, 114–115, 117
Constructive metatheory, 10–11
Constructivism:
  change/change resistance, 100–101
  chaos theory, application of, 99–100
  characteristics of, generally, 2–3, 9–10, 94–96
  cultural influence, 102–103
  emotionality, 95–96
  epistemology, 11
  experiential emphasis, 95–96
  infrastructure, 97
  integration, 96
  integrative, 27–28
  language of, 26
  philosophy, 94
  self and systems dynamics, 95
  teleology, 45–46, 97–100, 102
  therapeutic relationship, 101–102
  therapeutic techniques, 103–104
Control:
  locus of, 114
  schema, 62
Coping skills, 17, 50, 75, 81, 86

Index

Core constructs, 15, 28, 41–43, 49
Core ordering processes, 14–15, 135
Core themes, 133
Corey, Gerald, 29
Correspondence theory, 132
Creative power of the self, 12–13
Creative self, 12
Critical realism, 39
Cultural diversity, 29–30
Cultural influence, 102

Daily Record of Dysfunctional
    Thoughts (DTR), 85–86
Danger assessment, 81
Decatastrophizing, 82, 131
Deep structures, 14
Defense mechanisms, 63
Depression, 65
Depressive disorders, 129
Desensitization, 63–64, 131
Developmental psychology, 110
*Diagnostic and Statistical Manual of
    Mental Disorders,* 4th ed., 44
Diagnostic assessment, 44
Direct disputation, 64, 83, 131, 134
Discovery, 83
Distortion:
    clinical strategies, 74–75, 81
    labeling, 83, 131, 134
Distraction, 83, 131
Dodo bird effect, 93
Dormant schemas, 109
Dream(s):
    analysis, 131
    work, 76–77
Dreikurs, Rudolf, 72
Drives, 109
Duration of therapy, 79
Dynamic-humanistic-systemic-cognitive
    theory, 67
Dysphoria, 63

Early recollections (ERs), 41–42, 50,
    66, 75–76, 131
Eating disorders, 50
Eclecticism, 124–125, 134

Ecological approach, 42
Ego, 26
Ego defense mechanism, 63
Ellis, Albert, 94
Emotion, 41–42, 50–51
Emotionality, 95–96
Empathy, 22, 130
Encouragement, 10, 20, 24–25, 130,
    133
Energy models, 49
Environment, role of, 67
Epicurianism, 60
Epistemology, integration problem,
    124–127
Evidence, questioning, 82
Evolutionary epistemology, 39, 47–49
Evolutionary primacy, 103
Exaggeration, 83
Existentialism, 40, 119
Existential therapy, 2, 26
Expectancies, 17, 98
Experiential learning, 133–134
Experiential techniques, 45
Experimental work, 110
Explicit knowledge, 103
Extinction, 64

Fables, 64
Family constellation, 17–18
Family of origin, 42–43, 45, 50
Family system, *see* Family of origin
    approaches, 2
    influences of, 123
Fantasy, 17, 63–64, 83
Ferguson, Eva Dreikurs, 72
Fixed-role therapy, 45, 131, 134
Flooding, 63–64, 131, 134
Formal theory, 127–129, 134
Free association, 78–79
Freudian theory, 26, 41, 48, 60
Friendships, 18
Functionalism, 26–27, 40

Gestalt therapy, 26
Graded task assignments (GTAs), 82,
    84

Guided association, 83
Guided discovery, 131
Guilt, 63

Handbook of Cognitive Therapy Techniques, 64
Handbook of Psychotherapy and Behavior Change, 104
Heidegger, Martin, 108, 110, 113, 119–120
Heuristics, 124
Hidden text, 28
Holism, 39–40, 47, 49, 52, 94, 124
Homework, 80, 84–86
Hopelessness, 81
Human agency, 12–13, 109
Human sciences, 113
Husserl, Edmund, 108–114, 119–120

Id, 26
Ideal self, 15
Idiosyncratic meaning, 82, 131
Ihde, Don, 108, 110
Imagery:
  applications, 77
  replacement, 83–84
Implicit knowledge, 109
Implicit learning, 95
Implosion, 63, 131, 134
Information processing, 64
Insight, in Adlerian therapy, 23, 44
Instrumental schema, 62
Integration:
  defined, 124
  epistemology and, 124–127
  implications of, 1, 27–28
  present dialogue reflections, 127, 131–134
  theoretical, 125–126
Integrity, 103
Intelligence, 109
Intentionality, 39, 115
Intentions, 118
Internal working model, 18
International Association for Cognitive Psychotherapy, 94

Interpersonal awareness, 102
Interpersonal psychiatry, 26, 42, 50
Interpersonal relationship:
  attachment theory, 49–50
  development of, 42–43
Interpretation, 64
In vivo exposure, 84–85, 131

Journal of Cognitive Psychotherapy, 2
Journal of Individual Psychology, 10, 28, 31
Journal of Psychotherapy Integration, 95
Journal of Mental Health Counseling, 29–30

Kaam, Adrian van, 114
Kant, Immanuel, 11, 39, 108, 119–120
Kelly, George, 39
Kierkegaard, Soren, 107
Knowledge structures:
  general descriptions, 13–15
  selective attention, unity with, 16–17
  unconscious processes, 15–16

Labeling, 131–132, 134
Language, generally:
  acquisition, 73
  linguistic processing, 115
  significance of, 108
  skills, 111
Lazarus Multimodal Life History Questionnaire, 66
Learning process, 16, 110
Life narratives, 129
Life Style Inventory, 28
Lifestyle:
  analysis, 28, 44, 48, 51, 108, 131
  cognitive approach, 41, 101
  convictions, 61–62, 66
  defined, 41
  family of origin, 42, 45
  implications of, generally, 14–18, 21
  individuality of, 132
  meaning and, 40
  significance of, 20, 49, 72–73, 94, 101

Linguistic processing, 115
Locus of control, 114
Logic, 75, 134

Magic wand, 131
Mahoney, Michael, 94
Maladaptive schemas, 62, 67, 129, 131
Maladjustment, 19–21
Managed care, 2, 59
Manifestation, 61
Marital conflict, 65
Marx, Karl, 12
Maslow, Abraham, 114
Mastery, 64, 84
May, Rollo, 114
Meaning(s), 31, 40, 133
Meaning unit, 14
Memory, 16. *See also* Early recollections (ERs)
Merleau-Ponty, Maurice, 108, 110–111, 113, 116, 119–120
Metaphors, 14, 46, 64
Metatheory, 127–128, 134
Mind-body dichotomy, 27, 39–40, 51
Mirror time dialogue, 45, 131, 133
Modeling, 24, 64, 131, 134
Motivation, 98
Motivational schema, 62
Motor theory, 40, 110
Multicultural approaches, 29–30

Narrative psychology, 47
Narratives, 14, 133. *See also* Life narratives; Personal narratives; Self narratives
Narrative therapy, 9–10
National Institute of Mental Health (NIMH):
 function of, 59
 Treatment of Depression Collaborative Research Program (TDCRP), 65
Neo-Freudian approaches, 2, 26
Neurology, 119
Neurosciences, 109
Neurotic safeguarding, 95

Neurotic schema, 61
Nietzsche, Friedrich, 12, 107, 112–113
Nonconscious, 41
North American Society of Adlerian Psychology, 94
Novelty moderation, 131

Object relations, 26
Offspring theory, 126
Ontology-epistemology dichotomy, 39
Open systems, 99
Operant conditioning, 64, 131. *See also* Behavior modification
Options/alternatives, examination of, 82
Outcome research, 2

Paradoxical interventions, 64, 83, 101, 124
Participatory vitalism, 47
Partner selection, 18
Patient history, 79–80
Perception, 110–112, 115–116
Peripheral constructs, 41
Personal-cognitive organization, 103
Personal constructs, 61
Personal construct systems, 14–15
Personal construct theory, 47
Person-as-scientist metaphor, 46
Person-centered therapy, 2
Personal identity, 103
Personality disorders, 50, 65, 67, 96–97, 100, 129
Personality organization, 109
Personality style, 73
Personality theory, 110
Personal meaning organizations, 14
Personal narratives, 28, 47
PERSPACE, 66
Perspective, implications of, 116–117
Pharmacotherapy, 65, 82
Phenomenology, 38–39, 108–109, 113, 119
Philosophical roots, 11–12
Philosophical similarities:
 existentialism and meaning, 40

Philosophical similarities *(continued)*
  holism, 39–40
  phenomenology, 38–39
Physiology, 112, 119
Piaget, Jean, 99, 109
Pleasure ratings, 84
Postmodern theorists, 12
Posture, 117
Prigogine, Ilya, 99
Primary caregivers, 18
Proactive perspective, 21, 127
Professionalism, 92–93
Psychoanalytic theory, 26, 48, 92, 110
Psychodynamic approaches, 60–61, 67, 92, 126
Psychoeducational approaches, 2
Psychology of use, 40
Psychopathology, 19, 60, 67, 96
Psychotherapeutic techniques, 127, 131, 133–134
Push-button technique, 44–45, 131

Rational-emotive behavior, 41
Rational-emotive therapy, 2, 64
Rationalism, 94
Reactive perspective, 21
Reality therapy, 2
Real-life flooding, 64
Reattribution, 82, 131
Reciprocity, triadic, 50–51
Reductionism, 40, 97
Reflection, 115
Reflexivity, 134
Reframing, 85
Reinforcement, 97–98, 100, 102
Relapse rate, 104
Relational constructivism, 31–32
Relationship, in Adlerian therapy, 23.
  See also Therapeutic relationship
Relaxation training, 85
Religiosity, 30–31, 100
Reorientation, in Adlerian therapy, 23
Repertory grids, 45, 131, 133
Research studies, 27, 110–111
Resistance, 43. *See also* Change, resistance

Rogers, Carl, 22, 91–92
Role-playing, 84

Safeguarding, 43, 95
Sartre, Jean-Paul, 108, 110, 113, 118, 120
Scaling, 83
Schema, generally:
  development, 73–74
  focus, 79
  implications of, 41, 61
  theory, 61–63
Schema-focused therapy, 92
Selective attention, 16–17
Self, 114
Self-control, 64
Self-efficacy, 78, 81
Self-esteem, 43, 63
Self-evaluation, 62, 64
Self-help tasks, 82
Selfhood, 95
Self-ideal, 61
Self-in-process, 39, 49, 52
Self-instruction, 83
Self-narratives, 45, 131, 134
Self-organizing, 100
Self-protection, 21, 43, 95
Self-psychology, 26
Self-reflection, 133
Self-schema, 132
Self-worth, 43
Sensory functions, 40
Social constructivism, 2, 10
Social embeddedness, 17–19, 29, 42, 95
Social equality, 29–30
Social feeling, 42
Social interest, 24, 28, 42, 46–48, 77–78, 95
Social learning theory, 47, 50–51
Social skills deficits, 75
Social skills training, 84
Social support systems, 17
Society for the Exploration of Psychotherapy Integration, 93
Socratic questioning, 78, 83, 130

Solution-focused therapy, 133
Spirituality, 30–31, 100
Spitting in the soup, 44, 131
Stimulus-response, 110
Stories, 14
Streaming, 45, 131
Stream of consciousness, 134
Striving for perfection/significance, 45–46
Structuralism, 26–27, 48–49
Structural-functional dichotomy, 39, 49, 51
Style, implications of, 117–118
Style of life, *see* Lifestyle
Subjective-objective dichotomy, 39
Suicidal thinking, 81
Suicide attempts, 83
Superego, 26
Superiority concept, 45–46
Symbol creation, 17
Symptom, generally:
  focus, 79
  structure, 61
Systematic eclecticism, 124–125
Systematic pluralism, 125

Tacit knowledge, 41, 50, 95, 97–98, 103, 109
Target cognition, 64
Technical eclectics/eclecticism, 124
Teleology, 45–46, 97–100, 102
Teleonomic principle, 97–98
Teleonomy, 45–46, 97–100
Theoretical integration, 125–126
Theoretically progressive integration (TPI), 126
Theoretical similarities:
  Adlerian and cognitive therapies, 61–67
  Adlerian and constructivist therapies, 10–26
  cognitive approach, 41–42
  ecological approach, 42
  family of origin, 42–43
  overview, 40–41
  resistance, 43

Therapeutic alliance, 11, 22–23
Therapeutic change, 63–64
Therapeutic focus, 61–62, 74
Therapeutic relationship, 17, 21–23, 44, 61–63, 101–102, 125, 130
Therapeutic structure, 78–81
Therapeutic techniques, 44–45, 63–64, 75–77, 82–86, 103–104, 133. *See also* Psychotherapeutic techniques; *specific types of techniques*
Therapist-directed therapy, *see* Cognitive therapy
Therapist role, 63, 76, 78. *See also* Clinical strategies
Thermodynamics laws, 98–99
Thought-stopping, 83, 131, 134
Transactional analysis, 26
Treatment:
  conceptualization, 81–82
  protocols, 65
Treatment of Depression Collaborative Research Program (TDCRP), 65
Triggering schemas, 62
Trust development, 22, 44

Unconscious, 41, 109, 115
Unconscious processes, 15–16, 95
Underlying schema, 61
Unity, 16

Vaihinger, Hans, 108–109, 119–120
Validity, 127
Value system, 31, 40, 123
Voices, externalizing, 83

Wake up calls, 20
Well-being, influential factors, 40, 47, 73
What Life Should Mean to You (Adler), 31
Working alliance, 50
Work relationships, 18
Worldview, 62

Yalom, Irvin, 114
Young's Schema Questionnaire, 66

Zeitgeist, 1, 3, 32, 49, 91

 **Springer Publishing Company**

Clinical Advances in Cognitive Psychotherapy
Theory and Application
Robert L. Leahy, PhD, and
E. Thomas Dowd, PhD, ABPP, Editors

A virtual Who's Who in the field of cognitive psychotherapy! Briefly tracing the history and derivation of cognitive psychotherapy, the authors discuss its recent developments as an evolving and integrative therapy. Several of the chapters illustrate the applications of cognitive psychotherapy to treat such disorders as anxiety, depression, and social phobia. Other chapters discuss integration with therapy models such as schema-focused and constructivism. New empirically-based research is cited for treating the HIV-positive depressed client, the anorexic or bulimic sufferer, as well as applying cognitive therapy to family and group issues.

Partial Contents:

- Prologue: The Life of Aaron T. Beck, *M. Weishaar*
- History and Recent Developments in Cognitive Psychotherapy, *E. T. Dowd*
- Cognitive Models of Depression, *A.T. Beck*
- An Integrative Schema-Focused Model for Personality Disorders, *J. E. Young and M. Lindemann*
- Constructivism and the Cognitive Psychotherapies: Some Conceptual and Strategic Contrasts, *R. A. Neimeyer*
- Psychotherapy and the Cognitive Sciences: An Evolving Alliance, *M. J. Mahoney and T. J. Gabriel*
- Cognitive Therapy: The Repair of Memory, *K. Fleming, et al.*
- An Investment Model of Depressive Resistance, *R. L. Leahy*
- Cognitive Psychotherapy and Postmodernism: Emerging Themes and Challenges, *W. J. Lyddon and R. Weill*

2002   464pp   0-8261-2306-6   hard

536 Broadway, New York, NY 10012 • Fax: 212-941-7842
Order Toll-Free: 877-687-7476 • Order On-line: www.springerpub.com

Dual Relationships and Psychotherapy

Arnold A. Lazarus, PhD, ABPP and **Ofer Zur,** PhD, Editors

"The opinions expressed in this publication go directly to the challenges we will collectively face as we enter the 21st century."
— From the Foreword by
Patrick H. DeLeon, PhD, JD, ABPP
Past President, American Psychological Association

"This volume, through a series of diverse approaches and considerations, has dispelled for all time the monolithic notion that dual relationships are always harmful and should be avoided...remarkable and refreshing."
—**Nicholas A. Cummings, PhD, SCD**
Former President, American Psychological Association

This book challenges some of the basic "principles" of clinical codes of ethical conduct that have been established for psychiatrists, psychologists, and other mental health workers.

Partial Contents:
Part I. Overview and Controversies of Dual Relationships and Psychotherapy
Part II. The Ethics of Dual Relationships
Part III. Boundaries
Part IV. Laws, Boards, Ethics and other Forensic Matters
Part V. Dual Relationships in Special Populations
Part VI. Dual Relationships in University Counseling Centers
Part VII. Special Dual Relationships
Part VIII. Feminist Perspectives on Dual Relationships
Part IX. A Final Peek Behind the Scenes

2002   536pp   0-8261-4899-9   hard

536 Broadway, New York, NY 10012 • Fax: 212-941-7842
Order Toll-Free: 877-687-7476 • Order On-line: www.springerpub.com